Helps Keep the Devil at Bay

Presented to

_____

By

_____

Date

_____

Scripture references are from the Scofield Reference Bible, King James Version. Copyright © 1909, 1917: renewed 1937, 1945 by the Oxford University Press, Inc.

Used by permission.

Copyright © 2009

G.E. Crumbley, Sr.

All rights reserved under International Copyright Law. No portion of the publication may be reproduced, stored in a retrieval system, or transmitted in any form or by any means—electronic, mechanical, photocopy, recording, or otherwise—without the express written consent of the Author.

Photos by Author

Model for the cover and the divider photos: Author's granddaughter, Victoria Crumbley.

Dedication

This book is dedicated to my dear wife Norma, my 4 children, my 12 grandchildren and my great grandson, and to all those children who, I am sure, will be added to my family in the years to come. May God bless each and every one of you in a very special and generous way!

Introduction

God has blessed me so richly over the years by putting many Godly people in my life that have helped me to learn and to understand God's Word in a way that I could never have done on my own. One of these dear people was a truly wise woman in the knowledge of God's Word, and the one who led me to Christ, Mrs Willis Horton. What a blessing to have her as a friend for so many years. It's hard to imagine my life without the friendship of a dedicated servant of God, Dr. Jesse Hendley, who preached the Gospel from age 17 until his going home to be with his Lord in his 80's. The knowledge of God's Word this man shared was just awesome. Sitting under the teachings of a well known Atlanta pastor, Dr. Charles Stanley, for some 30 plus years has, no doubt, done more to grow me up in the Lord than I could ever imagine. This is a man God is using mightily in getting His message to the world. I wish to acknowledge with much appreciation that the ideas for some of these poems were inspired by his teachings. That lady preacher on TV, Joyce Meyer, that my wife began watching years ago, also infected me with her wisdom and knowledge of the Word and her unique method of teaching. Though I don't know her personally, her teachings have also inspired some of these poems. I am grateful to each of these men and women of God, and to God Himself for putting them in my path here on earth. This book may never have been written if not for the knowledge and insight into God's Word that I gained through them. God is so good!

It is my hope and prayer that these daily poems will encourage and inspire you and help you enjoy your life more fully. God's word is our instrument for helping keep the devil at bay and this book is full of and based on His Word.

The Author

A Rhyme A Day

Helps Keep the Devil at Bay

*for your daily
Inspiration and Enjoyment*

Dr. Gene Crumbley

January

January 1

On this very first day
Of a brand new year,
Rise up early and talk to God
And know that He will hear.
He will guide your every step
Your life is in His hands,
He has been through more than you
So you know He understands.
He is always on your side
On that you can depend,
And everything will work out
For your own good in the end.

Reference: Proverbs 8:17. Romans 8:28

January 2

God gives the grace to be humble
And He resists the proud,
We are to be clothed in humility
And not be boastful or loud.
Cast all your cares on Him
For He really cares for you
And be sober and vigilant
For Satan is coming after you;
He is like a roaring lion
Seeking whom he may devour
But if you're steadfast in your faith
You can resist him with God's power.

Reference: 1 Peter 5:5-9

January 3

Don't be anxious for anything
But let your needs be known
With prayer and supplication,
By the Scripture this we're shown.
Then the awesome peace of God
Which we can't understand,
Will come into our hearts and minds
For it is under God's command.
If we think on those things,
Paul said was honest, lovely and pure;
Things that were seen in him,
We'll have God's peace for sure.

Reference: Philippians 4:6-8

January 4

Jesus says He is the vine;
   The branches are you and I
And if we'll abide in Him
We'll bear fruit, by and by;
Branches can only bear fruit
When connected to the vine
And if the branches have no grapes,
There will surely be no wine.
If we don't trust in Christ
And try to live like Him each day,
We won't win many souls to Him
But just might turn a few away.

Reference: John 15:1-5

January 5

Trust in God with all your heart,
Not in works you understand,
And you will find good favor
In the sight of God and man;
Don't be wise in your own ways
But in all ways acknowledge Him
And He will direct your paths
To walk in light, not shadows dim.

Reference: Proverbs 3:5-7

January 6

Greater love has no man
Than he who lays down his life
For his friends like Jesus did,
While suffering pain and strife.
Jesus says we are his friends
If we do as He commands;
That shows Him we love Him
And know He holds us in His hands.
Christ proved His love for us
Dying there at Calvary,
So we could be in Heaven
And share His love eternally.

Reference: John 10:15-18; 15:13-14

January 7

We must live without hypocrisy
And shun things which are evil,
Then cling to those things good
And therefore defeat the devil.
We must be kind to each other
And show genuine brotherly love,
Then treat everyone with honor
To please our Heavenly Father above.
We must bless them that hurt us
And overcome their evil with good,
This will heap coals of fire on them
And they might change their attitude.

Reference: Romans 12:9-21

January 8

There was a certain rich man
Who was dressed in fine linen
And would give no food to Lazzarus;
He had plenty, so he was sinning.
Not even the crumbs on the floor,
That fell down from his table,
Would he give to this poor man
Covered with sores and disabled;
This beggar died and was carried
To the bosom of Abraham,
The rich man died and was buried
But went to Hades—He was damned.
This story goes much further
But ours will stop right there,
For it tells us if we're blessed by God
Our good blessings we must share.

Reference: Luke 16:19-23

January 9

God is our light and our salvation,
So whom shall we fear?
He also is our strength
And He is always near.
In our times of trouble
Why should we be afraid?
When our enemies come against us
God will come to our aid.
We know we belong to God
Through Jesus whom He sent
And who is with us everyday.
This should give us confidence.

Reference: Psalms 27:1-3

January 10

A good shepherd knows his sheep
He calls each one by name.
Jesus is our Good Shepherd
And for us He does the same.
When Satan, in sheep's clothing,
Comes and stands in our way,
Jesus is always there
To help keep that wolf at bay;
Christ gives to us eternal life,
We'll not perish you understand;
No man is able to pluck us
Out of His Father's hand!

Reference: John 10:14-29

January 11

If a man says he loves God
Whom he has never seen,
Yet, does not love his brother,
This is just not right it seems.
God says that man's a liar
For this much we do know,
A man who loves God
Will love his brother also;
And whoever shall confess
That Jesus is God's Son,
God dwells inside of him
And he in God—they are one.
God gave us this commandment,
That our brothers we must love,
Just as much as He loves us
As He looks down from above!

Reference: 1 John 4:15-21

January 12

Sometimes it takes just one word
Or spending time—a little while,
Or maybe a hug or a handshake
To make another person smile;
Will you do that for someone today?
To help bring them out of despair,
To show them they are loved
And that someone really cares?
This will help to cheer them up
And will lift their spirits too
But the one who'll be mostly blessed,
Will not be them—but you.

January 13

We know God so loved the world
That He sent His only Son
To hang and die upon the cross;
He sure got His *"job"* done!
Now anyone who believes in Christ
Will never, ever perish
But will have eternal life,
In Heaven with Him to cherish;
Christ did not come to condemn us
But that through Him we'd be saved;
When He shed His precious blood,
The road to Heaven was surely paved.

Reference: John 3:16-18

January 14

All those who are heavy laden
With worries and with stress
And burdened with many troubles,
Come to Christ, He'll give you rest.
Jesus Christ is very meek
And very humble in heart,
You'll find rest for your soul,
In Him right from the start;
As you learn from Him
To always do what's right,
You'll see His yoke is easy
And His burden is very light.

Reference: Matthew 11:28-30

January 15

Don't be deceived, God is not mocked,
What a man sows he will reap,
If he sows to his flesh,
Into his life bad things will creep.
The man who sows to the Spirit
Will reap life everlasting
And all his worries and woes,
On the Lord he will be casting.
Don't be weary in well doing
For God tells us in due season,
We shall reap and not faint,
God loves us; that's His reason.
Let us do *good* to all men,
Especially those of faith as we,
Then God will bless each effort
Put forth by you and me.

Reference Galatians 6:7-10

January 16

This truth is recorded for us
In God's precious Holy Word
We know it's absolutely true;
To not believe would be absurd.
It says God gave us eternal life
And that life is in His Son;
No other man could do that,
Jesus is the only one.
Those who know Christ have life;
The others they have not,
The ones that do will be in Heaven.
Is that a great promise, or what!

Reference: 1 John 5:11-13

January 17

Among the rulers in Christ's day
There were many who believed
But did not confess Him openly;
They were afraid of the Pharisees.
They knew they would be chastised
And be put out of the synagogue,
They all loved the praise of men
More than the praise of God;
Do not keep your faith a secret
But let it shine out brave and bold
And be a witness for Jesus,
By getting the Gospel message told.

Reference: John 12:42-43

January 18

Man looks on outward features
But God sees deep inside,
Things that man cannot see,
Those from God you cannot hide.
God sent Samuel to Jesse's house
To find a king among his sons;
Samuel would choose the tallest
But God said He's not the one;
He then looked at his brothers
And kind of liked what he saw
But God didn't want any of them,
He evidently saw a flaw.
But God had seen David's heart,
The young son out tending sheep;
Samuel anointed him to be king,
For his love of God was deep.

Reference: 1 Samuel 16:1-13

January 19

Blessed be to God our Father
Who gives us Mercy and Grace
And comforts us during troubles
And the tribulations we face.
He does this so we'll be able
To comfort others that we know
And do for them as He did for us,
As more like Christ we grow.

Reference: 2 Corinthians 1:3-4

January 20

Being born again of incorruptible seed,
That incorruptible Word of God,
Which lives and abides forever,
Not withering like grass or sod.
All flesh is much like grass
And the glory of man is like a flower,
Which soon dies and falls away
But God's Word has staying power.
Therefore lay aside malice,
Hypocrisy, envy and guile
And desire the milk of God's Word,
That you may grow—you are His child.

Reference: 1 Peter 1:23-25; 2:1-2

January 21

The believer is a new man in Christ
And cannot walk like other men
But must always speak the truth
And shun the appearance of sin.
He must not give in to the devil
Nor let the sun go down on his wrath,
But must always do that which is good
To those who come across his path.
He must be kind to others
And tenderhearted and forgiving,
Even as God has forgiven him,
Who like Christ, should now be living.

Reference: Ephesians 4:17-32

January 22

Now Christians may be different
From one another in many ways;
Sometimes it's in the things they eat
Or how they celebrate some days;
Also in how they worship
As they give the Lord their praise,
Some may shout and sing
While others their hands raise;
Many may sit quietly
In deep reverence and awe
But each of them is under grace
And not under any man's law.
Yet, in every true Christian
One thing remains the same,
Jesus died for each of us
And He took on all our blame.
So let's not judge one another
On things we may dispute
For each one who believes in Christ
Is God's child—that's absolute!

Reference: Romans 14:1-10

January 23

Listed here is a Promise verse
That the Author claims as his
And which he accepts from God,
Without question—without quiz;
If he will confess with his mouth
His Lord and Savior Jesus Christ
And believe God raised Him from the dead,
After He paid that awesome price;
His soul is forever saved
And now listen—this is *big;*
God has to keep His promise
There's no way He can renege!

Reference: Romans 10:9

January 24

The Lord is our refuge
Who made man out of dust;
He is our mighty fortress,
In Him we put our trust.
Under the shadow of His arms
He shields us from Satan's snares,
We need not be afraid
For God is with us everywhere.
No evil shall befall us
Because His angels are in charge
They have the power to protect us
And those powers are so large.
God says if we call on Him
He will answer and deliver,
And satisfy and give long life
Like a mighty flowing river.

Reference: Psalms 91

January 25

No temptation shall come to you,
Only that which is common to man
And you will be able to resist it
For your Lord God says you can.
He is faithful, and won't allow
More temptation than you can stand;
He will help you to bear it,
Yes, He'll lend a helping hand.
Beloved we are told by Christ
To flee from all idolatry
And keep sin out of our lives
And worship only God, and He.
We know that we can do this
For we read in Hebrews four fifteen,
That Jesus was tempted just like us
But He stayed pure and clean.

Reference: 1 Corinthians 10:13-14

January 26

To succeed in your Christian life
You must rely on the Holy Spirit
And truly trust in God's Word
And believe it when you hear it.
You must confess Christ as Lord;
Without ceasing you must pray;
You should attend public worships
And live like Jesus everyday;
Give freely without grudging
And live for others, not just you,
Witness to someone daily,
Not just one, but maybe two.
Keep growing in God's grace
And each day your Bible read,
God will honor your loyalty
And will meet your every need.

January 27

Godliness with contentment
Is really for our own gain;
Love of money is the root of evil;
We've all heard that refrain.
We brought nothing into this world
And will surely take nothing out,
So if we have food and raiment
We should be content—without a doubt.
The Godly man will flee worldly things
And follow after righteousness,
With meekness and faith and love
And with patience and godliness;
We should be more like Paul,
Content just where we are
And try our best to live good lives;
This beats all other living, by far.

Reference: 1 Timothy 6:6-11

January 28

The grace of God that brings Salvation
Has appeared to every man,
Teaching us to live soberly
And as righteously as we can;
We must deny ungodliness
No matter what shape or form
And forsake the things of this world,
Fruits of the Spirit should be our *norm*.
Look for that bless-ed hope
And the glorious appearing of Christ;
He sealed our Salvation at Calvary
When He paid that awesome price!

Reference: Titus 2:11-14

January 29

The fruit of the Spirit is love
And also joy and peace,
Gentleness, longsuffering, goodness
And great faith that's in our reach.
Then meekness and temperance,
Against which there is no law,
Is what we read in God's Word
And is the truth without a flaw.
The flesh was crucified in Christ
As were all affections and lusts,
So we should live in the Spirit
And walk with God in trust.
We should not desire vain glory
Nor provoke or envy another,
For His death on that old cross
Each of our sins did cover.

Reference: Galatians 5:22-26

January 30

God who at sundry times
Spoke to the fathers long ago,
By His chosen prophets
But in these times we know,
He speaks to us through His Word
And has appointed us His heirs
Of all things of this world
That with Jesus we will share.
In the brightness of His glory
He upholds things by His powers,
This man who had no sin himself
But gave His life to purge ours;
When He said, *"It is finished"*,
He sat at the right hand of God
And made a way for us to be there,
After life here on earth we've trod.

Reference: Hebrews 1:1-3

January 31

Praise God in His Sanctuary,
Praise Him in His awesome power,
Praise Him for the mighty acts,
He does every minute of each hour;
Praise Him for His greatness,
With trumpets and with harps,
Praise Him with stringed instruments
And do it from the heart;
Let everything that has breath
On earth and in Heaven above,
Praise the Lord, yes praise Him,
And give Him our hearts, and love.

Reference: Psalms 150

February

February 1

Every day we see changes
Nothing ever stays the same,
One day we're happy and healthy,
Next day there's sadness and pain.
But there is one thing we know
That will never, ever change
And that is our Lord Jesus,
Now to some that might seem strange.
Jesus was the same yesterday,
As He is today and will be tomorrow;
He can fill your life with joy
And help to ease your sorrow.
You only need to trust in Him
And His death at Calvary,
To have that abundant life
That He promised you and me.

Reference: Hebrews 13:8

February 2

Scripture says count it all joy
When you fall into temptation
And know the testing of your faith
Will increase it without question;
Let patience have her perfect work
That you may be perfect and entire,
Satisfied and wanting nothing,
Having no unfulfilled desire;
Blessed is he that endures temptation
That often penetrates like a knife,
For when he is tried he shall receive,
His promised golden crown of life.

Reference: James 1:2-12

February 3

Trust in the Lord and do good,
From these sayings do not part;
Delight in God and He will give you
All the desires of your heart;
Commit your ways to Him
By putting Him in charge
And He will bring it to pass
And your faith He will enlarge.
Those that wait upon the Lord
Shall this old earth inherit
And have peace and abundance;
This will be their gift of merit.

Reference: Psalms 37:3-11

February 4

Let every man be swift to hear
And very slow to speak,
Let him hold his wrath inside
With a will that's strong—not weak.
The angry man does not work
For God's righteousness,
So if a man holds his peace,
It's for his good, no less.

Reference: James 1:19-20

February 5

Don't remember former things
Nor consider things of old
For God will do a new thing,
This in His Word we're told.
He'll blot out our sins,
Which He sees down to the core,
And for His very own sake
He'll remember them no more.
God doesn't see those old sins
That we're prone to remember;
It's like in the spring we see
Those cold days of December;
So think only of the good things
That happened long ago
And they will bring you happiness
That's all you need to know.

Reference: Isaiah 43:18-25

February 6

Now bless-ed is the man
   Who walks not in ungodly counsel,
Nor stands in the way of sinners
Or sits in the seat of the scornful;
In the law of His Lord
This man finds great delight
And on this law He mediates
Each and every day and night;
He is like a tree by the waters
That will surely in due season,
Bear much fruit and prosper;
His love for God's law is the reason.

Reference: Psalms 1:1-3

February 7

God has chosen you dear Christian,
You are the seed of Abraham;
God is your mighty Lord,
He is your great "I Am".
Fear not He is with you,
Do not be dismayed,
He is your loving God
You must not be afraid,
He will strengthen you
In the times when you are weak
And He will give you comfort
As His loving grace you seek.
He'll uphold you with His righteousness,
In the grip of His right hand;
He is always there with you,
You are a part of His great plan.

Reference: Isaiah 41:8-10

February 8

May God be merciful to us
And bless each and everyone,
And cause His face to shine upon us
From sunrise to setting sun;
Let His people praise Him
And be glad and sing for joy,
God rules His people justly,
With them He does not toy.
When His people praise Him
The land will yield her best,
And those on earth will fear Him
And all the people will be blessed.

Reference: Psalms 67

February 9

Christ says love your enemies,
Those you do not like,
And bless those that curse you
Don't tell them to *"take a hike"*.
Do good to those who hate you,
Who use you and persecute;
These words are straight from Jesus
And are truths you can't refute.
If you love those who love you,
What will be your reward?
Most unbelievers do that
And they don't know the Lord.

Reference: Matthew 5:44-46

February 10

If any man be in Christ
A new creature now is he,
Old things are passed away
And all things are new, you see.
All things are now of God
To whom we are reconciled;
Each of us is His ambassador,
His own beloved child;
God made Christ to be sin for us
That we'd be made the righteousness
Of Jesus who knew no sin;
God gave us His very best.

Reference: 2 Corinthians 5:17-21

February 11

Obedience to God will bless others,
This you can understand,
Much like Peter, who obeyed Christ,
While standing on dry land.
Jesus told him to get in the boat
And push it out from shore,
Then cast his nets in a place
Where there were no fish before.
Now Peter had his doubts
But let his nets down anyway
And hauled in so many fish
He followed Jesus from that day!
We may not catch as many fish
As Peter caught back then
But we can do like Peter
And go out and fish for men.

Reference: Luke 5:1-11

February 12

Jesus said as my Father loved me
So I have loved you,
Continue in my love
And all my commandments do;
He said love one another
And let His joy fill your heart;
So live your life for Him
And let your love climb off the chart.

Reference: John 15:9-12

February 13

The Apostles looked toward Heaven
As Christ ascended in the air
And two men in white robes
Said why are you gazing there?
As you have seen Him taken up
In this manner He will return
And every true believer
For this event does yearn.
At His second coming
We will fly to our home above
Out of this old wicked world,
To God's place of eternal love

Reference: Acts 1:9-11

February 14

Now no man knows the day
    And no man knows the hour
That Heaven and earth will pass away,
No man has that power.
Two men shall be in the field
And one left and the other taken,
As will two women grinding corn,
Those left behind will be shaken.
They will try to explain away
The fact they've been rejected
By Christ at His second coming,
Something they had not expected.
That's why Jesus says be ready
For in that hour which you think not,
He will come to take home those,
Who believe in Him—His faithful lot!

Reference: Matthew 24:35-44

February 15

Fear of God is the beginning of knowledge
But fools hate wisdom and instruction;
A wise man will hear and learn;
Fools will fall into destruction.
If a son listens to his father
And heeds the advice of his mother
He will be wise in all his ways
And be blessed more than any other.

Reference: Proverbs 1:7-8

February 16

The Lord is our sun and shield,
   Who gives us glory and grace;
No good thing will He withhold
From those in His right place;
Blessed is the man, O Lord,
Who puts his trust in Thee
For you will give your blessings
To those who walk uprightly.

Reference: Psalms 84:11-12

February 17

Christ said His yoke is easy
For He bears our heavy load
As we travel on this earth
Along that narrow, weary road.
The burdens that we bear
All become so very light;
Christ pulls most of the weight
With His great strength and might.

Reference: Matthew 11:30

February 18

God has removed our sins from us
As far as the east is from the west
And His mercy is everlasting,
He wants for us the very best.
He has prepared a place in Heaven
For those who heed His call
And keep His commandments
For He loves them one and all;
His throne is there in Heaven
Set among those streets of gold,
Where He has full dominion,
And will let His love unfold.

Reference: Psalms 103:11-19

February 19

The just shall live by faith
 But if any man draws back,
God will have no pleasure in him
For great faith he does lack.
We must not be like those
Who draw back into perdition
But believe to the saving of the soul
And be in God's choice position.

Reference: Hebrews 10:38-39

February 20

The Lord is on your side
So whom shall you fear?
Man can do you no harm
As long as He is near.
The Lord will take your part
Along with those who love you;
He will take a strong hand
Against those that hate you too.
It is better to put your trust in Him
Than to have confidence in man,
For He is there in your distress
And for you He'll take a stand.

Reference: Psalms 118:6-8

February 21

These six things God does hate;
A proud look is one of them,
A lying tongue is another
For that really angers Him.
Shedding of innocent blood
And a heart of wickedness
And feet that run to mischief
That will lead a man amiss.
Number six is a false witness,
Then God adds number seven;
He is the man who sows discord
And has no place in Heaven.

Reference: Proverbs 6:16-19

February 22

Those whom God loves He chastises,
At present that doesn't seem good,
In fact, it sometimes seems awful,
Till the reason it's done is understood.
Later on it yields for us
The peaceable fruit of righteousness
And to those that endure it
God will give His very best.

Reference: Hebrews 12:6-11

February 23

The knowledge of sin comes by the law,
It shows us that we've done wrong
But Christ came to fulfill the law
That man had heeded for so long.
All men are justified by faith
Through Christ who was crucified;
All have come short of the glory of God,
That is why Jesus came and died.
We were justified by His grace
At that hour when it seemed
That we all would be lost forever
But by His blood have been redeemed.

Reference: Romans 3:20-24

February 24

There is great cloud of witnesses
About us whose numbers are huge;
We must lay aside sins that beset us
As we seek God's refuge.
We must run the race before us
With much patience within, without,
We need to remain confident
And be free of any doubt.
Jesus Christ is the author
And finisher of our faith,
Who for the joy set before Him
Endured the cross and sealed our fate.
We know He did it just for us,
Despising the shame He bore alone;
He now intercedes for each of us
On the right hand of God's throne.

Reference: Hebrews 12:1-2

February 25

Ask and it shall be given you,
Seek and you shall find,
Knock and the door will open;
Just keep that in your mind.
If you ask you shall receive
And you will find what you seek
And the door will be opened;
(Knock boldly, not so weak.)
Who of you would give a stone
To a son who asked for bread?
Or to a son who wanted fish
Would give him a snake instead?
If we, being evil, know how to give
Our children gifts as we should,
How much more will our Father above
Give to us things that are good.

Reference: Matthew 7:7-11

February 26

The scriptures say herein is love,
Not just that we love God
But that He loved each of us
Before we even had a *"bod"*;
He that sent His only Son
To be full payment for our sin,
Will one day because of His love
Send Him back to earth again.
Beloved, if God so loved us,
We ought to love one another,
Because God says if you love me
You should also love your brother.

Reference: 1 John 4:10-21

February 27

When we are troubled on every side
We should not be distressed,
When we are persecuted
We must not feel depressed.
Though we be down trodden,
We should never be dismayed
For we have a loving God
So we should never be afraid.

Reference: 2 Corinthians 4:8-9

February 28

O Lord, our God, how excellent
Is thy name in all the earth
Who sets thy glory above the heavens
And who gave Adam birth.
When I consider the heavens,
The work of thine own hands,
And the moon and stars
Then I say what is man,
That you are mindful of him
Whom you made lower than the angels
Then crowned with glory and honor
And showed love from every angle.
You made him to have dominion,
You put all things beneath his feet,
You planned for his Salvation,
Thereby making his life complete.

Reference: Psalms 8:1-9

March

March 1

Christians must abstain from evil
And even the appearance of it,
Or we might cause someone to stumble
And Christianity would *"take a hit"*.
Other eyes are watching you
As you do your daily routine
And your actions will be criticized,
I'm sure you know what I mean.
Do not give ammunition
To the enemy to knock you down;
Just live your life the way you should
To let them know you're Heaven bound.

Reference: 1 Thessalonians 5:22

March 2

The righteous ones cry out
And their Lord God hears.
He takes away their troubles
And He removes their fears.
He is always near to those
Who are broken hearted,
And are of a contrite spirit,
From them He won't be parted.
For each one who loves Him
He will redeem their soul
And if they'll only trust in Him
He will make them whole.

Reference: Psalms 34:17-22

March 3

The prayer of faith shall save the sick
And the Lord shall heal them;
If anyone has committed sins
They shall be forgiven him.
The effectual fervent prayer
Of a righteous man availeth much,
Like those of the prophet Elias
Who prayed and got in touch
And asked God in earnest
To withhold the dew and rain
And it didn't even drizzle
Until he prayed again!
So when you pray in earnest,
And are intently fervent too,
God will answer your prayer
If it's in His will for you.

Reference: James 5:15-18

March 4

Christians should, as newborn babes,
The milk of God's Word desire,
That it would nourish our souls
And raise our spirits higher.
Pray that it would help us grow
So we could get down to the meat
Of God's Word like Paul did
And pass it on to those we meet.

Reference: 1 Peter 2:2

March 5

In the book of Isaiah,
Those pages of God's Word,
It says have you not seen
And have you not heard?
That the everlasting God
The Creator of the earth
Does not faint or get weary
But gives strength to those of worth;
Those who wait upon Him shall
Mount up with wings as the eagle,
They shall run and not be weary,
(It's in His Word—it's legal).
They shall walk and not faint
For their strength will be renewed,
There is no searching His understanding,
No need for it to be reviewed.

Reference: Isaiah 40:28-31

March 6

A merry heart is good for the soul
But by sorrow the spirit is broken,
A soft answer turns away wrath,
Angry words are best not spoken.
The tongue of the wise is knowledge,
A wholesome tongue is a tree of life
But the perverse tongue of the wicked
Just stirs up trouble and strife.
So keep your thoughts clean and happy
And let the words from your lips be right,
Then you will bring joy to others
And you'll sleep really well at night.

Reference: Proverbs 15:1-13

March 7

If a man doesn't offend in word
God says he is mature
And able to control his tongue
So his words all come out pure.
We put bits in horses' mouths
To guide them and they obey
By turning their whole body;
We should control our tongues this way.
Even those great big ships,
The ones driven by strong winds,
Are controlled by a small rudder
And they reach the port again.
Our tongue is like that small rudder
That steers that great big ship;
We need to control it at all times
And try to never let it slip.

Reference: James 3:2-6

March 8

God has given us eternal life
And that life is in His Son;
No one else can do that for us,
Jesus is the only one.
These sayings are for those
Who believe on Jesus' name
And **know** they have eternal life;
They will never be the same.
To etch this in your heart and mind
Choose yourself a promise verse,
Then when you have any doubts,
Use it those doubts to disperse.

Reference: 1 John 5:11-13

March 9

God said if you obey His laws
He'll give you rain in due season,
The fields will yield good crops,
Your obedience will be the reason.
You will thresh till the grapes come in
And they will last till time to sow,
You'll eat your bread until you're full
And dwell safely always, you know.
He'll give you peace in all the land
And at night when you lie down
You shall not be afraid
He'll not let your enemies come around.

Reference: Leviticus 26:3-7

March 10

There is just one lawgiver
　Who is able to save and destroy,
We must not judge one another
For that is the devil's ploy.
We should not say today
That tomorrow we'll go to a city
And stay there a year or so
To buy and sell, what a pity;
Who knows what tomorrow holds
Or even the remainder of this day?
Life is much like a vapor
That stays awhile then fades away.
When you say I'll do this or that
And you don't want to be surprised,
You had better say, *"If the Lord wills"*
And maybe, *"If the creek don't rise"*.

Reference: James 4:12-15

March 11

Jehoshaphat feared the Lord
   And proclaimed a fast in the land,
He set himself before the Lord
To seek His helping hand;
He said, Lord of our fathers
Are you not the God in Heaven?
The one who rules the earth,
Even the kingdoms of the heathen;
In your hand is there not power
And also not great might,
That none can stand against you
And defeat you in a fight?
We now stand before you Lord
Our eyes are fixed on thee,
Because we don't know what to do,
Protect us from our enemy.
They didn't fight the battle alone
For God said, do not be dismayed,
Just go out to your enemy
And fight—don't be afraid.
God was right there with them,
(In God's Word it's written),
The people sang praises to the Lord
And their enemies were smitten.
When Jehoshaphat was bewildered
And didn't know what to do
He put all his trust in God
And we must do that too.

Reference: 2 Chronicles 20:3-22

March 12

A man went down to Jericho
And fell among some thieves,
He saw a certain priest come by
And must have felt relieved;
That man didn't help him
And neither did a Levite;
Another man soon came along
Who took time to do what's right.
He helped this man in need,
He was that Good Samaritan;
We should be more like him
And help others when we can.

Reference: Luke 10:30-37

March 13

What does it profit you?
My brother and my friend
If you have faith and not works
Can faith save you in the end?
If there is one who is destitute,
Naked and without food
And you say depart in peace
You'd be so unkind and rude;
For them to be warm and full
You should give them what they need,
That is where your works come in
As you do this good deed.
James spoke so very clearly
In the scripture when he said,
If you have just faith alone,
Without works your faith is dead.

Reference: James 2:14-20

March 14

A persistent widow went to a judge
Who wouldn't see her right then,
So she continued to seek his help
By going back again and again;
She wanted justice from him
Against a man, her enemy,
And he finally heard her story;
He said she keeps bothering me.
Won't God do the same for us,
We who are His chosen ones,
And listen to our persistent pleas,
Then answer them through His Son?

Reference; Luke 18:3-7

March 15

Jesus was teaching in a house one day
And He was also healing the sick.
A paralyzed man was brought to Him
But the crowd was much too thick.
His friends took him to the housetop
And through a hole in the roof
Lowered him down to Jesus,
Who knew this was living proof,
That they believed He could heal him
And rather than lying in bed,
Once Jesus said the word
He'd get up and walk instead.
Jesus forgave his sins right there
And the man got up and walked;
He trusted Christ completely
And his disease came to a halt.

Reference: Luke: 5:17-25

March 16

There is a time for everything
For everything there's a season,
A time to be born and a time to die;
Only God knows the reason.
There's a time to build and tear down,
A time to laugh, and one to weep,
A time to throw something out
And there's also a time to keep.
There is a time to shut up
And bring a conversation to an end,
Sometimes that time to shut up,
Is before any talk begins;
Everything is beautiful in its time
And everything God does endures,
Nothing can be added or taken away
All gifts from God are clean and pure.

Reference: Ecclesiastes 3:1-14

March 17

On His way to Jerusalem,
Between Samaria and Galilee,
Jesus was met by ten men
Who all had leprosy.
They stood at a distance
And cried out in a loud voice,
Asking Jesus to heal them,
Hoping He would make that choice.
Christ told them to go see the priests
And on the way all ten were healed
But just one came back to thank him,
The other men's lips were sealed.
When God does good things for us
We should have a grateful attitude,
Like this man with leprosy had
And show Him our gratitude.

Reference: Luke 17:11-16

March 18

A man gave a great supper
And invited many friends to come
But they all gave him excuses,
They must have been so dumb.
They let the things of the world
Rule over their hearts and minds
So the man invited strangers
And the friends were left behind.
That certain man represents God,
The great supper, eternal life,
The invitation was to accept the Lord,
The Lord and Savior, Jesus Christ.
Those friends missed God's blessings;
That should be a lesson to me and you,
Not to let worldly things distract us
And cause us to lose His blessings too.

Reference: Luke 14:16-24

March 19

Blessed is the man who fears God
And who walks in His ways,
He will eat the fruit of his labor
And be happy all of his days.
His wife will be as a fruitful vine
Growing by the side of his house;
His children will gather at his table
With him and his wife, (his spouse);
The Lord will bless this man
Just like He blessed Israel
And because of his love of God
His family will be blessed as well.

Reference: Psalms 128

March 20

If Adam and Eve had obeyed God
In Eden where it all began
And not eaten the forbidden fruit
Today there would be no sin in man.
The world would be a perfect place
In which we all would live,
There would be brotherly love
And not one sin to forgive.
There would be peace, not war,
And no such thing as being wrong;
Each man would do what was right
Everyone's faith would be strong.
But Adam and Eve disobeyed God
So He did the very best thing,
He put His Son, Jesus, on the cross
And on that day did bring,
Perfect love to an imperfect world,
What a great and wonderful plan;
We are justified by His blood,
Down to the very last man!

Reference: Genesis 3:6; Romans 5:9

March 21

All Christians should be waiting
For their Savior to return
And keep oil in their lamps
Ready to light and burn,
Just like those five wise virgins
Ready to meet the bridegroom,
Not as those foolish five
Who were kept out of the room.
We must always be prepared
For He'll come as a thief in the night
And we won't be left behind
Because of His death we have that right.
We'll be there with the Bridegroom,
Our Lord and Savior Jesus Christ,
Who paid the ransom for our sins
For no one else could pay that price!

Reference: Matthew 25:1-13

March 22

Let not your heart be troubled,
If you believe in God believe in me,
In my Father's house are many mansions,
Christ said that to us, you see.
If it weren't so I would have told you;
I go to prepare a place, and when I do,
I'll come and receive you to myself
That where I am, you'll be too!

Reference: John 14:1-3

March 23

When the fig tree puts out its leaves
We know that summer is near,
The winter and spring is behind us,
The Holy Bible makes that clear.
This generation shall not pass
Till things predicted are fulfilled,
Wars, pestilence and earthquakes,
Yet, God's Word will linger still.
The Heaven and earth will pass away
But as the flood in the days of Noah
So shall the coming of Christ be,
In God's own time—not before!

Reference: Matthew 24:6-7, 32-39

March 24

Jesus is the way
 And He is the truth,
He also is the life
And He is the living proof,
No man comes to the Father
Except by Jesus Christ, His Son;
If you know Him, you know the Father,
They are the same, they're one.
He said believe me, I *am* in the Father;
And the Father in me, (it's true),
If you don't believe me by my words
Believe me by the works I do.

Reference: John 14:6-11

March 25

Christians must not get caught up
In the bad things of this world,
We should enjoy the good things
But avoid the evil Satan hurls.
There are some good things on TV,
Yet, it must cause God concern
When Christians watch shows daily
But they do not discern,
That most are filled with cursing,
Sex, lying, cheating and greed,
Infidelity, hate and anger
And that's not what our minds need.
We must keep our minds on things
Which are wholesome clean and pure,
That honor God in thought and deed
Then He will bless our lives for sure.

March 26

David said when I'm afraid
I will put my trust in thee
And I will have no fear
For Lord you are there with me.
My enemies cannot hurt me,
There is nothing they can do
Because in order to get to me
They will have to come through you.

Reference: Psalms 56:3-4

March 27

If you scold a scorner he'll hate you
But a wise man will show love,
These words from the book of Proverbs
Are straight from the Lord above;
Give instruction to a wise man
Then he will be wiser yet
And if you teach a just man
More learning he will get.
All our days are multiplied
And the years of our lives increased
As we walk in the ways of God,
This will cause Him to be pleased.

Reference: Proverbs 9:8-11

March 28

Having faith is a different ball game
When you're the one that's hurting,
When you've lost your job
And you don't know for certain,
How you can pay your bills
Or put food on your table,
It's easy to say have faith
When your own life is stable,
But it gets tough at times
To maintain your Godly trust
And not give in to Satan
However, that's a must;
When folks say have faith,
They may at times sound pious,
Yet, they are filled with empathy
As they run those words by us.
Yes, it's a different ball game
When things in your life seem dark
But if you let Christ in the game
He'll knock Satan out of the park!

March 29

God's eyes are on the righteous
And His ears are open to them,
He will hear your prayers
So tell your needs to Him.
If you suffer for righteousness sake
You should be happy and not sad
And be grateful to God
For this opportunity you've had.
Sanctify God in your heart
And be able an answer to give
To those who ask for the reason
Of the hope in the life you live.
If anyone speaks evil of you
Just trust God and be calm,
This will reflect Christ's love in you
And will be like a soothing balm.

Reference: 1 Peter 3:12-16

March 30

Hear me when I call, O Lord,
God of my righteousness,
Have mercy on me
And soothe me in my distress.
O sons of men just how long
Will you let your vanities deceive?
And turn God's glory into shame
Just as if you don't believe?
Don't you know the Lord, Himself,
The Godly man will choose
And when that man calls on Him
His prayers won't be refused.

Reference: Psalms 4:1-3

March 31

This is the generation of Jesus
Beginning with Abraham,
Then Isaac, who was spared
When God provided a ram;
Isaac had Jacob, who had Judas
And in between were many others,
A man named Obed had Jesse,
The father of David and his brothers;
Still more were begotten after him
Some with odd names that varied,
Until we finally come to Joseph,
The man God chose for Mary.
When he saw she was with child
He was going to put her away
But God told him not to do it
And his Lord he did obey.
Those are the generations of Christ
And it finally comes down to us
For we each are children of God,
Through the sinless blood of Jesus!

Reference: Matthew 1:1-25

April

April 1

God says He is my Shepherd
And to want I shall not,
He makes me lie down
In a green and grassy spot;
He leads me beside the waters,
Not moving but so still
And He restores my soul
And my spirit He does fill.
He leads me on the right paths
For the sake of His Holy name;
Through Death Valley's shadows,
I shall walk and not be lame,
I shall fear no evil
For God is there with me,
His rod and staff gives comfort
In the face of my enemy;
He anoints my head with oil
And my cup shall overflow;
His goodness and mercy follows me
All the days of my life, I know.
I will dwell in the house
Of my Lord God forever;
He'll be there with me always
And leave me, no not ever.

Reference: Psalms 23

April 2

The hairs on your head are numbered,
God knows every single one
Because you are His adopted child,
Through Jesus Christ His Son;
He tells you not to be afraid
And not to be down trodden,
You're more valuable than a sparrow;
That small bird He's not forgotten.
He will not forget anyone
Who confesses Christ before men
And He'll confess them to the Father
Who is the Christian's next of kin.

Reference: Luke 12:6-8

April 3

God's law is perfect and converts
The soul that in sin lies;
His testimony is most sure
And it makes the simple wise.
The laws of God are right
And cause rejoicing in the heart;
His commands are all pure
And light to the eyes impart.
Unspotted is the fear of God
That does endure forever;
His judgments are all true,
They are righteous altogether.
More than fine gold they are
By His children to be desired;
They are sweeter than honey
And they are much to be admired.

Reference: Psalms 19:7-10

April 4

Heaven is God's throne
And the earth is His footstool;
He made them and man
Over whom He has sole rule.
God looks for the humble man
Who has a contrite spirit
Who fears Him and loves His Word
And who really wants to hear it.
You may be that very one
That God wants to use,
So if and when He calls on you
You must not dare refuse.

Reference: Isaiah 66:1-2

April 5

First, you must love God
With all your heart and soul;
Second, love your neighbor,
It will help to make you whole.
Let love fill your heart
Until it does overflow,
Then do good for strangers
And others that you know;
If you give yourself to others
And do for them your best,
You will please God very much
And your own life will be blessed.

Reference: Mark 12:29-31

April 6

Isaiah saw a vision
Of the Lord upon His throne,
His angels were there also;
Isaiah's sins were made known.
He said "Woe is me",
My lips are so unclean,
As are those of my people
For the Holy King I've seen.
Isaiah heard the voice of God
Saying whom shall I send,
Who will go for us
And spread my Word to men.
Could you be God's "Isaiah"?
The one who hears Him call
And say to Him send me,
I'll take your Word to one and all.

Reference: Isaiah 6:1-8

April 7

How excellent in the earth, Lord,
Is your Holy name!
Your glory is so far above
The starry skies you framed.
When I look to the heavens
There always will remain,
The sun, the moon, the stars,
That your hands did ordain.
David says, what is man
That he is remembered by thee
Or what is the son of man
That so kind to him you'd be.
You made him a little lower
Than the angels we are told
And then with glory and honor
You crowned his head with gold.
How excellent in all the earth,
O Lord is your Holy name:
Let us praise you in our hearts,
As your great wonders we proclaim.

Reference: Psalms 8:1-9; 9:1

April 8

God could have sent His angels
With drawn swords in their hands
To save Jesus from facing death
But that wasn't in His plans.
God loved every man so much
He knew they would be worth
Every drop of Jesus' blood
That splattered on the earth.
Christ would give His life for all
And do it of His free will;
Even though men were evil
He'd do it for them still.
Christ could have called those angels
To save Him from that cross
But didn't do it just because,
Man forever would be lost.

Reference: Matthew 26:52-56

April 9

God says your thoughts are not my thoughts
And your ways are not mine,
As the heavens are higher than the earth
So are my ways higher than thine.
As the rain comes from above
And at times the pretty snow,
The earth receives their water
And it helps the seeds to grow.
So shall God's Word go out
And void it won't return;
It shall accomplish what He wills,
To help His people live and learn.

Reference: Isaiah 55:8-11

April 10

Make a joyful noise unto the Lord
And serve Him while being glad
Come into His presence with singing
And be happy, don't be sad.
Know that the Lord is God,
By Him we have been made
And like the sheep of His pasture
He finds us when we've strayed.
Enter His gates with thanksgiving
And into His courts with praise
Be thankful and let Him know it
As our voices we all raise.
The Lord is good and merciful
And His kindness is so pure;
His faithfulness and truth
For all generations will endure.

Reference: Psalms 100

April 11

A man who sows sparingly
Will also reap that way
But a man who sows bountifully
Will reap a good crop someday;
Let every man so give
As he purposes in his heart,
Not grudgingly or of necessity,
For that would not be smart.
God loves a cheerful giver
And His grace will abound
With favors and earthly blessings
And someday a Heavenly crown.

Reference: 2 Corinthians 9:6-8

April 12

Jesus said Father forgive them
 For they know not what they do,
As He was being crucified
Giving His life for me and you;
If He could do that on the cross
While in such agony and pain,
We should be able to forgive others,
It would be for our own gain.
We need to respond like Jesus,
Who dwells in Heaven up above,
And forgive those who hurt us
And show them unconditional love.

Reference: Luke 23:34

April 13

John says herein is love
  Not that we loved God
But that He loved us first
As on this earth we trod.
He sent His only Son
To be payment for our sins
And if we confess Him as Lord
Eternal life right then begins.
Now, if God loved us that much
We must love each other
And let His love be perfected in us
So, His love, others will discover.

Reference: 1 John 4:10-14

April 14

Do not attempt to rob God
By keeping tithes and offerings
But take them to His storehouse
Otherwise you'll be in sin.
He'll open the windows of Heaven
For He is the Lord of Host
And He'll pour out His blessings,
More than enough to make you boast.
You'll be so richly blessed
You won't have room to receive it
And He'll do this just for you
If you will just believe it!

Reference: Malachi 3:8-10

April 15

Learning is a good thing
It helps keep your mind alert
And staying in God's Word
Is the best effort you can exert.
Just memorize a promise verse
And lock it in your mind
It will help you get thru each day
Much easier, you will find.
Then you'll always have an answer
That will be a fact, not a feeling,
For the hope that's in your heart;
That verse will send old Satan reeling.

Reference: Proverbs 1:5; 1 Peter 3:15

April 16

Job was a righteous man,
Who walked in God's ways,
There was no one else like him
And God blessed all his days.
Then old Satan came along
Seeking whom he could destroy
And God gave Job over to him
And Satan took away Job's joy.
He gave Job many boils
And killed his children—all ten,
But Job wouldn't curse God;
He suffered but wouldn't sin.
God doubled Job's possessions
Because he never lost his trust
And kept his faith in God;
What a great lesson for us.

Reference: Job 1:1-22; 2:1-8; 42:12-13

April 17

An angel came to Gideon
Then sat down under a tree
And said, O man of valor
The Lord is here with thee.
Gideon said if that is true
Why has this happened to us?
Where are God's miracles?
Somehow it doesn't seem just.
Surely God has forsaken us
And put us in the enemy's hands;
The angel told Gideon in God's might
He would save Israel, (God's land).
But Gideon didn't feel qualified
He felt weak and much resigned
And did not have his confidence,
That's when God gave him a sign.
When God decides to call on us
And we don't feel adequate
Just remember He is with us,
To help us do His job first rate.

Reference: Judges 6:11-17

April 18

The people marveled when they saw
A man speak who once was mute
And the maimed made whole again;
A blind man's eyesight made astute.
Seeing the lame man walking
On legs so strong and stout,
They glorified God and Jesus
Who brought those miracles about.
All this was done in just one day
So the people would believe
That Jesus was the Son of God
And their doubts were all relieved.
Now if you have doubts
And your faith is somewhat blurred,
You don't need a miracle,
You need to get into God's Word.

Reference: Matthew 15:29-31

April 19

Yours, O Lord, is the greatness
And the Glory and the power,
All in Heaven and earth is yours,
Your majesty is like a tower.
Riches and honor come from you
And you reign over all;
In your hand is power and might,
You give strength to those that call.
Therefore we thank you God
And praise your Holy name;
We know everything comes from you,
Including all honor and fame.
We are just strangers here
On this earth and nothing more,
Our days are like shadows
As were our father's here before.
Let us, O Lord, give back to you
With a willing and cheerful heart,
Even more than you want from us,
Let us do more than our part.

Reference: 1 Chronicles 29:11-15

April 20

Jesus said the Kingdom of Heaven
Was like a net cast into the sea
And when it was dragged to shore
It was as full as it could be.
It had things of every kind,
The bad mixed with the good;
The bad was thrown away
And the disciples understood,
That at the end of this age
Angels would come down
To separate the evil from the just
And choose who will wear a crown.
Those who don't know Jesus
Will be thrown into a lake of fire
But those who do believe in Him,
A Heavenly home they will acquire.

Reference: Matthew 13:47-50

April 21

A woman who was a Gentile,
With her daughter, demon-possessed,
One day went to see Jesus
And stood before Him and professed,
Have mercy on me, O Lord,
But Christ kept silent, (not one peep),
His disciples wanted to send her away
But He took time for this one sheep.
He told her it was not good
To throw children's bread for dogs to eat
But the woman said even little dogs,
Eat crumbs at their master's feet.
Jesus then said to her
Woman your faith is *great*
And He healed her daughter at once,
Not at some later date.
This woman was one of the people
That had *great faith* of this kind;
Another was the Centurion, who said,
Say the word and he'll be fine.
When we read of their great faith
And those miracles Jesus did,
We must also show our great faith
And not hide it under a lid.

Reference: Matthew 15:22-28

April 22

This is really the confidence
We should have in God each day,
That if we ask anything in His will
He will hear us when we pray.
If we know He hears us,
We know He'll perform His task
And answer our petitions
And give us what we ask.
We must go boldly to His throne
While praying on bended knee
And believe He'll provide those things
That He wants for you and me.

Reference: 1 John 5:14-15

April 23

There were people in Jesus' day
Who thought He was a good man;
That He came to set an example
But they did not understand.
They denied He was the Messiah,
Especially the Pharisees and Scribes,
But Jesus knew their thoughts;
He picked up on their "vibes".
One day He asked His disciples,
Including Peter, so devout,
Who they thought He was
And Peter let out a shout;
He said, Lord you are the Christ,
The Son of the living God,
Who came down from Heaven
Upon this earth to trod.
Though Peter would deny Christ
Before the crowing of a cock,
His faith was very strong,
It was as solid as a rock.
Jesus saw Peter's loyalty
And knew He would be able
To build His church on Peter's faith,
That was so strong and stable.
Our faith should be like Peter's
It should not bend or waver
And God can use us to win souls
That is what our Lord would savor.

Reference: Matthew 16:1-18

April 24

How we handle adversity
Shows how much faith we have;
Little faith can result in fear
While great faith is like a salve.
When those storms in life arise
That causes our boats to rock,
Great faith will ease us through the pain;
We're tied safely to God's dock.
Yes, we will all face problems
At some point along life's way
But if you know who's in control
It will keep your fear at bay.

Reference: Mark 4:37-40

April 25

Those who don't know Jesus
Believe He was just a man,
Going around doing good
But every Christian understands,
That His purpose was more than that,
He came down to earth to die,
Because no man could resist sin
No matter how hard he'd try.
That's why Christ left Heaven
And hung upon that cross,
He put our guilt on His shoulders,
Otherwise we would all be lost.

Reference: John 11:49-52

April 26

The Kingdom of Heaven is like a merchant
Who seeks after beautiful pearls
And when he finally finds one,
Sells all he has in this world.
He then goes out and buys it,
This great pearl, this precious one
Because to him it's priceless;
It is likened to God's Son.
This story gives us a picture
Of our Savior, Jesus Christ;
We are His pearls of Salvation,
He bought us at an awesome price.

Reference: Matthew 13:45-46

April 27

God had pity on Nineveh
And sent Jonah down we're told,
To give them God's warning
And help save thousands of souls.
Jonah had no pity for them
And would have let these people die.
They didn't know right from wrong,
So he had to be God's ally.
God taught Jonah a lesson
While in the belly of the whale,
One we need to learn ourselves;
When God speaks, do not rebel.

Reference: Jonah 1, 2

April 28

Now Jesus is the best friend
That one can have, by far,
And even though we're sinners
He accepts us where we are.
He knows we face hardships
For He faced everyone we face.
He had very few possessions
And for a home He had no place.
Jesus cares for all who suffer;
He suffered for them on the cross.
I hope He is your best friend
For without Him you are lost.

Reference: John 15:13-15

April 29

God's kindness never ceases,
His compassion never fails,
They're fresh and new each morning
And each noon and night as well;
He will comfort and guide you
And encourage you in your life;
He's trustworthy and dependable
As you go through your daily strife.
God is omniscient; omnipotent
And we also know that He
Is omnipresent always,
That should make us worry free.

April 30

When David was a small lad
  His job was tending sheep
Out in his father's pastures,
It's the way he earned his keep.
David always depended on God
Like when he killed the giant so tall,
He did it with God's help
And didn't hesitate at all;
When God calls us to do a job
We must just hop to it
And always depend on Him
To show us how to do it.

Reference: 1 Samuel 17:48-51

May

May 1

When you're in a hurry
And you know God's not
You need to just relax
And praise Him for what you've got.
Spend some time in His Word,
Talk to Him on bended knee;
He'll provide what's good for you
Just you wait and see.
If your hope is for that thing
That at present can't be seen,
Just have the patience of Job
And keep your thoughts clean.
We must not try to rush God
For He has His own time
And if we'll just wait on Him
Everything will turn out fine.

Reference: Rom 8:25; James 5:11

May 2

When you see those junkyards
With wrecked cars all around
They're as ugly as they can be
Until snow comes falling down.
Snow soon covers everything,
The junked cars and debris
And those ugly junkyards
Become beautiful sights to see;
That is how God sees us,
He doesn't see our junk you know,
For Christ's blood washed away our sins
And it made us as white as snow.

Reference: Isaiah 1:18

May 3

Faith without works is dead
According to the book of James,
You must look out for your neighbor,
Not to do so is a shame.
If you see your fellow man
Is hungry, or maybe chilled,
You must be willing to help him,
Not just say be warmed and filled.
Christians are left on this earth
To help others and to serve,
God makes it easy for us;
He even gives us the nerve.

Reference: James 2:14-17

May 4

On those cold wintry days
When you wish you had a fire
To take the chill out of the air,
Something your heart would desire.
Just pull up your comforter
And lay back in your recliner,
Then you'll be nice and warm
And nothing could be finer.
Jesus did just that for us
When He sent the Holy Spirit down
And He is now our Comforter;
His warmth and peace abounds.

Reference: John 14:16-18

May 5

God says two can't walk together
Unless they agree as one
And that applies to you and me
So we must see that it's done.
We need to stay in God's Word
And even go that extra mile
In order to be pleasing to Him;
He's our Father—we're His child.

Reference: Amos 3:3

May 6

When you feel your faith is weak
And could use a "shot in the arm"
Read Hebrews chapter eleven
It will encourage you like a charm.
When you see the faith of Abel
And that of Enoch and Noah
And the faith of Abraham
It will make your own faith soar.
Many others are named in there,
Joseph and Moses are just two
Who had great faith and were blessed
And God will do the same for you.

Reference: Hebrews 11

May 7

You know the story of Thomas
Who doubted Jesus was alive
And did not change his mind
Till he saw Christ when He arrived;
We can't see Christ like Thomas did
But through faith we can believe
That Jesus died and rose again
And we'll not have been deceived.

Reference: John 20:24-29

May 8

Very early in the morning
Two Mary's went to the grave
To rub Christ's body with oil
And some spices they had made.
They saw the grave was open
Not closed up by the stone,
There was no sign of Jesus,
Not a trace of skin or bone.
Two men in white robes
Filled their hearts with dread
When they asked them why
They sought the living among the dead?
This is part of our proof today
That Jesus Christ has risen,
That He broke the bonds of death
To save us from Satan's prison.

Reference: Luke 24:1-6

May 9

Jesus loves us each so much
And this is how we tell
He opened His arms so wide
His hands stretched from nail to nail.
Now, if He really needed to
He would do it all again
But His death was once for all;
His blood covered every sin.
His arms still are open wide
To welcome and save all
But you have to believe in Him.
It's up to you to make that call.

Reference: Hebrews 9:27-28

May 10

Don't be like those Pharisees,
Who lived in Jesus' time,
They did things just for show
Their faith wasn't worth a dime.
They were righteous on the surface
But way down deep inside
Not one thing was done for God
But just to satisfy their pride.
So please do not be pious
Looking down on your fellow man
But do all things to serve God
And do good each time you can.

Reference: Luke 11:39-44

May 11

We know God is the Potter
And we are the molded clay,
Let's take pride in our bodies
For God made us all this way.
Our bodies are the temples
In which the Holy Spirit dwells,
We must take good care of them;
We must love ourselves as well.
We should also love our brothers
For that is the best way,
For us to draw God's favor
And receive His blessings every day.

Reference: Isaiah 64:8; 1 Cor. 3:16

May 12

Micah prophesied that Bethlehem,
A city that was very small,
Would be the birthplace of Jesus
Who would reign over one and all.
He would stand and feed His flock,
This great shepherd, Christ the Lord,
And give His life for His sheep
And pay for our eternal reward.
Micah's prophesy came true
For that *is* where Christ was born
And we still celebrate His birth
Each year on Christmas morn!

Reference: Micah 5:2-4

May 13

God is *not* the author
Of chaos and confusion,
So do not listen to Satan
Or he will create that illusion.
We need to stay in God's Word;
Not just read, but meditate,
Then God will surely bless us
And our days will turn out great.

Reference: 1 Corinthians 14:33

May 14

The Books of the Old Testament
Are Genesis, Exodus, Leviticus,
Numbers, Deuteronomy, Joshua
Then Judges, Ruth and thus,
First and second Samuel
First and Second Kings;
Two Chronicles and Ezra
Then Nehemiah and Esther are seen.
There's Job, Psalms and Proverbs,
Ecclesiastes, and then next;
Solomon, Isaiah, Jeremiah,
And the Lamentations text;
Ezekiel, Daniel and Hosea,
Are followed by Joel and Amos
And Obadiah, and then Jonah,
Who made that whale famous!
Micah, Nahum, Habakkuk,
Zephaniah and Haggai,
The words of Zechariah;
Ending up with Malachi.
These Books of the Old Testament
Are listed here in rhyme
If you study them carefully
You'll learn all thirty nine.

May 15

You must never give up,
If you fall along life's way;
Get back up and try again
And you will be okay.
You only fail when you quit
And don't try anymore.
So trust God and keep trying
And He'll open up a door.
You must run the race before you,
You must fight a good fight,
Just like Paul says in the Bible
And everything will be alright.

Reference: 1 Cor. 9:24; 2 Tim. 4:7-8

May 16

Christ will set His sheep on His right
And on His left He'll set the goats,
The sheep are ones who believe in Him;
They'll wear robes; long white coats.
They'll inherit the kingdom God prepared,
From the foundation of the world;
The goats are unsaved people who,
Into a lake of fire will be hurled.
If you know Christ, you are His sheep
And He now controls your fate.
If you don't, accept Him now
And you'll enter those pearly gates.

Reference: Matthew 25:33-46

May 17

Delilah didn't trick Samson,
She asked him what to do
To bind him and afflict him
And this should have been his clue.
He really tricked her three times
Because he lied and got away;
Now if he had just stopped there
Everything would have been okay.
But no, he told her what to do,
She must cut off his long hair,
He knew she planned to harm him,
So he sure messed up there.
Sometimes Satan tempts us,
Not just once or twice,
So do not listen to him!
That's really sound advice.

Reference: Judges 16:4-20

May 18

Jesus told all the people
 They didn't seek after Him until,
They ate the bread He provided
And their stomachs were all filled.
He said don't seek meat that perishes
But seek that which endures;
Seek the eternal life in Heaven,
That God has sealed, and now insures.
Do we seek after food that fills?
Or after His righteousness,
Think about it for a while
Then do what you think best.

Reference: John 6:26-27

May 19

A Pharisee passed a man in need
And later so did a Levite;
They would not stop and help him
Scripture says that is not right.
Christians should always help
Though it may take a while
But that time will be well spent,
If it turns a frown into a smile;
Christians should have compassion
And just like that Samaritan
Be willing to help others
Each and every time they can.

Reference: Luke 10:31-34

May 20

We tend to think of Peter's failures,
So this truth may seem remote;
We should think of his successes,
Like when he got out of that boat.
He walked on water for a while
Before he began to sink,
The only man but Christ to do that;
It took great faith, don't you think?
We should be more like Peter
And have the courage to step out,
Then do what God tells us to do,
Even though we have some doubts.

Reference: Matthew 14:28-30

May 21

On Patmos John saw a vision
Like the Son of man, who said,
I am the first and the last,
I now live who once was dead.
Christ shall live for evermore,
He has eternal breath
And all men should believe in Him
He holds the keys to Hell and death.
He holds the keys to Heaven also,
Where all men desire to be;
If you know Him as your Savior
You'll be there—yes Sir-ree.

Reference: Revelation 1:9-18

May 22

John told the people he was *not* Christ
But was a forerunner to Him,
Not worthy to tie His sandals
But was to preach about Christ to them;
Some still thought he was Jesus
But he was not the "Bridegroom",
He was more like the "Bestman"
Who must step back and give Christ room.
John said, He who comes from above
Will surely be above all
And he who believes in God's Son,
Lives forever; for heeding His call.

Reference: John 3:28-36

May 23

When Peter followed Jesus,
He loved Him with all his heart
But he still did a few things
That didn't seem so smart.
He said he would die for Christ
Then he denied Him thrice,
Using some real bad language;
That certainly was not nice.
But we know Peter loved Him
For after Christ was denied
Peter went out of the temple
And he very bitterly cried.
At those times when we are weak
And don't stick up for our Lord,
We must ask for His forgiveness
And get back in one accord.

Reference: Matthew 26:70-75

May 24

King Ahab angered God more
Than all kings before him had;
When he married Jezebel
This made the Lord so mad.
Ahab then built an altar
On which he would worship Baal,
That's when God sent Elijah
To this evil king to tell;
That He would stop the dew and rain
For three years, and this is why;
So Ahab would know He was God
And believe in Him when things got dry.
Ahab later repented
And he gained God's respite.
We see humility sure works wonders
To make things turn out right.

Reference: 1 Kings Chapters 16 thru 21, various Verses

May 25

God gives blessings to His children
But how many they receive,
Will be up to each person
And how deeply they believe;
When God blesses someone
It means He will intervene
And help them act in such a way,
That His goodness will be seen;
The fullness of His blessings
Will come and will be steady
If we do what we can do
To let God know we're ready.
We first must recognize
He is the source of everything
And blesses us in our troubles
And in the heartaches they bring.
We must listen to God
And tune in to Him always
Seeking guidance and direction
That will help us through our days.
We must not only listen to God,
We must obey Him, that's a fact,
And trust Him for everything,
Just the way a Saint should act.
We must wake up each morning
Expecting God's best that day
And do our best to please Him,
By doing all things His way!

May 26

Christians serve the Living God,
Whose name is Jehovah,
We are His through His Son,
Jesus Christ, who made us over;
He's the one we received
As our Lord and Savior;
He renewed our hearts and minds,
Our thoughts and our behavior;
We are new persons in Christ;
He changed our lives, our ways
And if we submit to His will
He will bless us all our days.

Reference: 2 Corinthians 5:17-18

May 27

After Elijah told King Ahab
God would hold back rain and dew,
The word of God came to him
And told him what he must do.
He was to go to a city and hide
By a brook where he could drink;
God would send ravens to feed him
And he didn't know what to think.
But when the brook dried up
Because there was no rain
God sent him to a widow's house
And there he was sustained.
Elijah trusted God completely
And did exactly what He said.
God then supplied all his needs,
That included his daily bread.

Reference 1 Kings 17:1-9

May 28

Shortly after Moses died
It soon came to pass
That God spoke to Joshua,
For the first time, but not the last;
Now that Moses was dead
Joshua must arise and go over
The Jordan to the Promised Land,
In the open not under cover.
God would be there with him
But he must be bold and strong.
He must keep the law as Moses did
To possess the land for which they longed.
God gave that land to Joshua
Because he was bold and unafraid
And trusted God with all his heart,
So God's plan was not waylaid.

Reference: Joshua 1:1-5; 3:7

May 29

God stopped the river Jordan,
That was overflowing its banks;
This God who was all powerful
And to whom they all gave thanks.
Priests took the Ark of the Covenant;
And stood in the river, but stayed dry,
Then all the people crossed over,
This is the truth, it is no lie.
God dried up the Jordan River
He stopped its mighty flow,
So all the people on the earth,
Including you and I would know,
That God who was with Moses
Was there with Joshua too
And if we believe and trust Him,
He'll be there for me and you.

Reference: Joshua 3:7-17

May 30

Elijah called everyone together,
All the people of Israel,
For God wanted to prove to them
That He was alive and very real.
There soon would be a battle
Between Him and the idol Baal
It would turn out good for God
But Baal wouldn't fare so well.
The people cried out to Baal
To burn their sacrifices with fire,
They begged, pleaded and cut themselves
But Baal didn't answer their desires.
Elijah then built an altar to God,
He used twelve big stones,
He laid wood and a bullock on it
And the truth would now be known.
Water was poured on the altar
One time, two times, then three
And God then sent His fire
So these people all could see,
That He was the only true God
The most Holy One above,
The people now worshipped Him;
They showered Him with their love.

Reference: 1 Kings 18:25-39

May 31

Every Christian needs a promise verse
To help them be reassured
That they have eternal life
And help make them feel secure.
John three sixteen is such a verse
That is famous and well known
And the one my daughter, Jennifer,
Claims as her very own.
It says God so loved the world
That He gave His only Son
(He had no other child;
Jesus was His only one.)
It says whoever believes in Him
Will not surely ever perish
But have everlasting life,
(In Heaven with Him to cherish).
If you don't have a promise verse
Do yourself a great big favor,
Claim one as your very own
And your faith will never waver.

Reference: John 3:16

June

June 1

After King Ahab told Jezebel
Elijah killed her men with a sword,
She then threatened to kill him
And he lost faith in his Lord.
Elijah fled to another city
And he hid out in a cave;
He was afraid of Jezebel
And not being very brave.
The Word of God came to him
In that cave where he lodged
And said why are you hiding?
(His duties he had dodged.)
Elijah said the children of Israel,
God's covenant had forsaken
And all of His prophets slain
(So his faith was now shaken).
God sent him to a mountain
And He sent a very strong wind,
Also fire and an earthquake
That He, Himself, was not in.
At times God sends an earthquake,
Or at times a small still voice
To encourage us to trust Him
It's up to us to make that choice!

Reference: 1 Kings 19:1-12

June 2

Joshua met an angel,
In the form of a man,
On the road to Jericho,
With a sword in his hand;
This man blocked his pathway,
Standing there like a post
And said he was a captain
Of the Lord God's Host;
Joshua fell and worshipped him,
After taking off his shoes,
And later went on to Jericho
To fight a battle he wouldn't lose.
Joshua knew he had stood
In God's presence on Holy ground
So when he fought against Jericho,
His faith was strong and sound!

Reference: Joshua 5:13-15

June 3

When Jesus washed the disciple's feet
He was giving them an example,
That they should be humble
But His lesson was not ample,
For Peter did not understand
And said you'll not wash mine;
Christ said He'd have no part with him
And that troubled Peter's mind;
He wanted Jesus to wash his feet
And even his hands and head,
For if he had no part with Jesus
He would just as soon be dead.
Christ was showing the disciples,
How to be humble and to serve,
People that they knew and loved
And also others they observed.

Reference: John 13:1-15

June 4

When the day of Pentecost came
The Apostles were in one accord;
Suddenly there came a great sound
Like a mighty wind from the Lord,
It filled the house where they were
Like cloven tongues of fire
And they received the Holy Ghost
Because that was God's desire;
People around them were confused
For when the Apostles spoke the words,
Each man heard in his own tongue
And to them this seemed absurd.
These Apostles were Galileans
And seemed to be drunk with wine
But Peter said they were not drunk
And the words of Joel he opined.
He said God would pour out His Spirit
And like Jesus they'd now behave,
Then it would soon come to pass,
Those who called on Him would be saved.

Reference: Acts 2:1-21; Joel 2:28-32

June 5

Christians are children of God
Through the blood of Jesus,
Who died upon that cross
To pay the ransom for us;
We're redeemed through His blood
According to God's pleasure
Whose love, mercy and grace
Is endless, without measure;
Christian's all know the truth,
Christ died for our Salvation
And we fellowship with him
Through prayer and supplication.

Reference: Ephesians 1:5-13

June 6

Those that walk, the walk of faith
  And have made with God a truce,
Will avoid false doctrines
That Satan uses to seduce.
They will shun hypocrisy
And refuse profane fables
And exercise true Godliness,
For in Jesus they are able;
They'll trust in the Living God,
Who is the Savior of all men
And know that it is on His grace,
Not on works, that they depend.

Reference: 1 Timothy 4:1-16

June 7

Before the ascension of Jesus,
(This is Luke's admission),
Christ spoke to His Apostles,
Giving them the Great Commission;
He told them they'd have power
When the Holy Ghost came on them
And they would be His witnesses
Throughout Judea and Jerusalem;
They'd take His Word to Samaria
And the uttermost parts of the earth
And those who believed in Him
Would have a second birth;
That commission applies today
To each one of God's Saints;
We must be His witnesses
And not refuse or say we can't.

Reference: Acts 1:8

June 8

God made each of us alive
Who were dead in trespasses and sin
And walked according to the world,
Spiritual death would be our end.
We were children of disobedience
And by nature children of wrath
But God in His rich mercy
Reached down and changed our path.
He has raised each one of us
So we can sit together,
Someday in Heaven with Jesus
And dwell with Him forever.
We are all His workmanship
Created in Him to do good,
By His grace, not by our works;
Is that clearly understood?

Reference: Ephesians: 2:1-10

June 9

Our Christian leaders face attack
For they serve on the front lines,
Like Peter when Satan attacked him
And he denied the Lord three times.
What about King David,
A man after God's own heart,
Who Satan tempted with Bathsheba
And he did something not so smart.
Noah found grace in God's eyes
And built the ark and all was fine
But then Satan tempted him
And he became drunk with wine.
Great men like Jonah and Moses
Were also tempted and deceived
And did awful things against God
And yet they still believed.
Christian, you're on the front lines
Many people are watching you,
So Satan will tempt you also
With all the evil he can do.

June 10

Just make sure the works you do
   Are done for the right cause,
That they are done to glorify God,
And not seeking man's applause.
When you do your good works
Do not sound a trumpet loud
For that will be your reward,
Showing others you are proud.
God will reward things done for Him
But those done for self He trashes
And they'll be burnt up in fire
And be just a bagful of ashes.

Reference: Matthew 6:1-4

June 11

O Lord, you are my hiding place
And you are my shield;
I have hope in your Word
Which I know is very real.
Keep evil doers from me
As I try to keep your laws
And hold me so I'll be safe,
While working for your cause.
Yes Lord, you're my hiding place,
A safe haven in the storm,
I know you will protect me
As my character you form.

Reference: Psalms 119:114-117

June 12

Your Word is a light unto my path
  And a lamp unto my feet,
I will keep your righteous judgments;
To my taste those words are sweet.
Your testimonies I have taken
As a heritage to me forever;
They cause rejoicing in my heart
That will leave me, no not ever.

Reference: Psalms 119:105-112

June 13

There was a certain woman
With an issue of blood twelve years;
She spent all her money on doctors
And probably shed many tears.
She had heard of Christ's miracles
And came to Him from behind;
She reached out and touched His robe
And Jesus perceived this in His mind.
He knew power had gone from Him
And turned to this woman so bold
And told her that her faith
Is what really made her whole.
This woman believed in Jesus
And knew she would be healed;
We should strive for faith like hers,
For that's *what sealed the deal!*

Reference: Luke 8:43-48

June 14

Love of money is the root of evil,
In the scripture this we're told
And many people covet it;
Some would even sell their soul.
It causes some to lose their faith
And often brings great sorrow
Because they seek it diligently,
Today, tonight, tomorrow;
God says we all can be rich
In good works and righteousness,
Using our money for His good
And we'll be greatly blessed.

Reference: 1 Timothy 6:9-11

June 15

God is our refuge and our strength
A very present help in trouble,
Therefore we will not fear
Even though those troubles, double.
Though the waters of the earth roar
And though the mountains shake,
The Lord of Host is with us
And will stay there for our sakes.
Be still and know that He is God
And He wants a close relation;
Since you are His child through Christ,
He wants your praise and adoration.

Reference: Psalms 46

June 16

When Philip went to Samaria
He preached Jesus Christ to them
And most were in one accord
And paid close attention to him.
They listened to the truth he spoke
And saw miracles performed,
Like calling out demon spirits
And having lives transformed.
Joy filled that whole city
As the palsied and sick were healed;
The people then learned about Jesus
And that their Salvation was sealed.
We too, can witness like Philip,
Yet not cause quite as much fuss;
Just talk to people one on one
And tell them each about Jesus.

Reference: Acts 8:5-8

June 17

Titus said the people were foolish
And disobedient and deceived,
Living in lusts and pleasures
But found Jesus and believed.
Then the love and kindness
Of their Lord and Savior appeared,
Not by something they had done;
Titus made that very clear.
It was by God's own mercy
And His love so abundantly
That they became heirs of God;
They would be His eternally.

Reference: Titus 3:3-7

June 18

An angel of the Lord told Philip
To go south and he did as told
And on his way to Joppa
An Ethiopian he did behold.
He was a man of authority,
This eunuch who served his queen
And was reading Isaiah's words
But didn't understand, it seems.
Then Philip was led by the Lord
And went over to him and said
Do you understand what you're reading?
He said no, and maybe shook his head.
Philip climbed into the chariot
And explained Isaiah's words;
Christ was being led to slaughter
And he believed what he heard.
Philip told this man that Jesus
Was God's one and only Son;
The eunuch was then baptized
And was pleased at what he had done.
God then transported Philip
Right then to another place;
Where he boldly preached the Gospel
To another people face to face;
Philip won many souls to Christ
And he did something very rare,
When God sent him to another place,
He flew there through the air.

Reference: Acts 8:26-40

June 19

Philemon's servant, Onesimus,
Robbed him then fled to Rome.
Paul converted him in prison
And then sent him back home;
Paul thanked Philemon for his faith;
For loving the Lord and the Saints,
And asked him to take Onesimus back
And do so without restraints.
Paul wrote all this to Philemon
And also told him in this letter,
If he'd let Onesimus return to him
It would surely be much better.
For Paul was old and needed help,
Yet, he sent Onesimus back
Hoping his master would tell him,
To turn around and re-trace his tracks;
Paul said if he has wronged you
Or owes you any amount,
Please forgive him of his debt
And put it on my account.
Christ did just that for us
When He died at Calvary,
Our charges were put on His account
So we could be debt free.

Reference: Philemon 1:1-19

June 20

A man named Simon used sorcery
And thought he was so great
But when compared to Philip
He was really second rate.
The people who heard Philip
Believed and were baptized,
Simon, himself, also believed
And everyone was surprised.
So Simon continued with Philip
And was very much amazed,
At the miracles and signs
Which Philip did in those days.
When Peter and John laid hands on some
They were filled with the Holy Ghost,
Then Simon wanted that power too
And offered money to his Hosts;
Peter said it cannot be bought
And you are evil in God's sight
You must repent of your wicked ways
And pray that God will make it right.
Simon was thinking only of himself;
He wanted the praise of men.
If we have that same attitude
Our wicked ways we should amend.

Reference: Acts 8:9-22

June 21

Titus tells us that a deacon
Should be the husband of one wife
And his children should be faithful,
Not causing grief or strife.
The deacon must be blameless
And be a good steward for God,
Not self-willed, short tempered, greedy,
Or a lazy man He has to prod.
He should be hospitable
And temperate, just and sober;
He must be of sound doctrine
In order to win others over;
God's Words he must hold fast
The ones he, himself, was taught
And not be like false prophets
Whose words all go for naught.
All those things listed above
Is what a good deacon should be
And if we want to serve God,
They should apply to you and me.

Reference: Titus 1:7-9

June 22

There was a woman named Tabitha,
Who God raised from the dead:
He didn't do this by Himself
But used Peter in His stead.
This is how it came about,
She was full of good deeds,
Always doing for others;
Helping them meet their needs.
It came to pass one day
That she got sick and died,
So the disciples sent for Peter
Who came quickly to her side.
Some widows stood there weeping,
Holding clothes that she had made
And Peter sent them all out
Then knelt down and prayed.
He then turned to her body
And told Tabitha to arise
And she sat up right away,
After opening up her eyes;
He took her hand and lifted her
And showed them she was alive.
This was spread though-out Joppa
And preaching of the Gospel thrived.
Many people believed in Christ
Due to this woman with a big heart,
Who Peter raised from the dead
For doing much more than her part!

Reference: Acts 9:36-42

June 23

The Galatians lost their blessings
For they lived under legality,
That is, living under the law
That kept them from being free.
They didn't know that law and grace
Could not ever co-exist,
Otherwise they might have chosen
Not to live their lives like this.
Ishmael represented the law
For he was born after the flesh
But Isaac was born through grace
And those two will never mesh.
Christ is of the lineage of Abraham,
Therefore, Christians are under grace.
For His blood shed at Calvary,
Fulfilled the law and took its place.

Reference: Galatians 4:15-31

June 24

After he baptized the eunuch
Philip was taken up in the air
Because his job was finished
And God needed him elsewhere.
Philip was one of three men
That God caused to fly.
The others were Enoch and Elijah;
Someday it could be you and I.
We Christians look forward to
Being taken up by our Lord,
In the air at His second coming;
This will be part of our reward.

Reference: Acts 8:39-40

June 25

Each cute and cuddly baby
That we love with all our heart
Knows what's good from bad
Almost from the very start;
When they reach out their hand
For something they shouldn't touch
They *know* they're in trouble
They just don't know how much.
The Bible says we're born in sin
Because of Adam and Eve,
Who disobeyed God in the garden
But some find that hard to believe.
Yet if those babies grow up
And never lie, cheat or steal,
Or break any other of God's laws,
That would surely be unreal
But they would *still* need Jesus
The one who paid the cost
Of their sins with His blood
When He hung upon the cross!

Reference: 1 Cor. 15:22; Romans 3:23-24

June 26

The Holy Spirit is our Comforter
And He is our helper too;
He helps us know right from wrong
And discern what's false from true.
The Holy Spirit is our teacher,
Who reminds us of God's Word
And allows us to put into action,
All those truths that we've heard;
He's the one who comforts us
When things don't go our way
And convicts us of our sins
As we live from day to day.
Thank God He loved us enough
To let His Spirit live in us,
To help guide us in this life,
Once we've accepted Jesus.

Reference: John 14:16-18; 15:26

June 27

Wives submit to your husbands,
That's what God says you must do
For he is the head of the wife
And he must watch over you.
As Christ is the head of the Church
And the Church to Him subjected,
So is the wife to her husband;
He must be loved and respected.
Husbands must love their wives
Just as Christ loved the Church
Being gentle and protective
Never leaving them in the lurch;
A man leaves his father and mother
To be joined to his wife as one
And if they're grounded in God's Word,
Their marriage can never be undone.

Reference: Ephesians 5:22-33

June 28

Christ is the believer's role model,
We should be more like Him,
So the earth will be a better place,
A happy place—not grim!
We should love one another,
Always being good and kind,
Trying to please each other
And be of one like mind.
We should humble ourselves,
Like Christ we should obey
Each and every command
That God chooses to send our way.

Reference: Ephesians 4:32; 5:1-2

June 29

Children obey your parents
For God says this is right.
Honor your mother and father
And you'll be precious in His sight.
God says if you do this
All will be well with your soul
And you will live a long life.
As His blessings all unfold.
Fathers don't provoke your children
Or cause them to have wrath
And they will love and honor you,
(You need to do your math)!
If parents and children do God's will
From the bottom of their hearts,
They'll have a close knit family
Unlikely to be torn apart!

Reference: Ephesians 6:1-6

June 30

Believers are the salt of the earth,
Christ said this from The Mount
But when salt loses its flavor
It becomes of no account.
Our actions and deeds as Christians
Work that very same way,
We can win souls to Jesus
Or can keep some souls at bay.
Let your salt retain its flavor
By doing things good and pure
And others will see Christ in you
And you'll be used by God for sure.

Reference: Matthew 5:13

July

July 1

Jonah didn't obey God's call
  In fact, he turned and ran,
He thought he could outrun God
But found out no one can.
He was in the belly of a whale
For three long days and nights
But then he learned his lesson
And began to set things right.
He went straight to Nineveh
And many souls were saved
We too had better heed God's call
And do what's right—not misbehave.

Reference: Book of Jonah

July 2

Jesus called His disciples together,
All twelve of them if you please
And gave them the mighty power
To heal people who had disease.
The first to come was Peter,
Next was his brother Andrew
And two brothers, James and John,
Then Philip and Bartholomew;
Thomas came there also
And Matthew, the Publican,
James, son of Alphaeus,
And Thaddeus were on hand.
Simon of Canaan, and Judas,
(The disciple who would betray),
All gathered to hear Jesus
Give them His orders, and obey.
He told them to go forth
To the lost sheep of Israel
And tell them the Kingdom of Heaven
Was at hand and very real;
He told them to freely give
Of what God had freely given,
So it would motivate these people
And to the Lord they would be driven.
This is also our call from God
To go out into the world
And let everyone know about Jesus
Each man, woman, boy and girl!

Reference: Matthew 10:1-8

July 3

Man thinks riches, honor and glory
And good works will satisfy
And Satan surely deceives them
Making them believe that lie.
A man can have many houses
And vineyards by the score;
He can have gardens and orchards
And fruits and crops galore.
He can have many servants,
Including pretty maids
And lay up a lot of treasure
With all the money he has made.
Whatever his heart desires
From himself he won't withhold
And because of his great vanity
He will reward himself tenfold.
Yet, when he does reflect
On the things that he has done
And his labor to achieve them
And the fame and honor won,
It all seems so meaningless
Like chasing a wild wind;
Only those things done for God,
Will satisfy him in the end!

Reference: Ecclesiastes 2:4-11

July 4

Elijah was taken up in the Spirit
And set down by God in a valley
In the midst of so many bones,
The number he could not tally.
As his spirit passed among them
He saw they all were dry;
God said can they live again?
He answered, you know Lord, not I.
God said say O dry bones
Hear the word of the Lord,
I'll put the breath of life in you
And you'll become a living horde.
Then I'll put flesh on you
And muscles and sinew
Then cover it all with skin,
Your bodies I will renew.
There came a great rattling noise
As those bones came together,
They were fully clothed in skin
That was as tough as leather.
Yet, there was no life in them
Not a single one had breath,
Till the four winds blew on them
And brought them up from death;
When we feel our bones are dry
And we need our spirits restored,
We know God has that power
So we must trust in our Lord.

Reference: Ezekiel 37:1-14

July 5

Jesus was brought before Pilate
Who asked, are you King of the Jews?
Christ wanted to know if this
Was a name that he did choose?
Pilate said to Him your people
Have delivered you to me
So what is it you have done?
That is what I ask of thee.
Christ told him that His Kingdom
Was not of this old world,
If it were, angels would fight for Him;
(His victory banner would be unfurled).
Pilate again said to Him,
Tell me, art thou a king?
Jesus said to him once more,
It is you who says this thing.
To this end I was born
And to this cause I came
That I bear witness of the truth;
(Things will never be the same).
The people then chose Barabbas
And Jesus was condemned
They didn't believe He was God
So they would have no part of Him.
When we ourselves have to choose
Between what's good and evil,
Don't choose Barabbas—choose Christ,
And you'll defeat the devil.

Reference: John 18:33-40

July 6

Hypocrites are those people
Who praise God with their mouth
And honor Him with their lips
But their hearts have headed south.
They are not close to God
And worship Him in vain.
They live ungodly lives
And from God's words abstain.
They are the blind leading the blind,
So just let them alone
For if they do believe in Christ
It surely is not shown.

Reference: Matthew 15:7-14

July 7

Jesus says we're the salt of the earth,
We know that salt gives flavor
And that it is good for nothing
Once it has lost its savor.
So if we don't let others see
What a Christian life is all about
And influence them to follow Christ,
We've lost our savor, no doubt!
So don't go through your life
Like a worn out bag of salt.
Be a good witness for Jesus
And bring Satan's antics to a halt.

Reference: Matthew 5:13

July 8

Jesus went to another land
　Down in the Galilee region
And saw a man with demons,
So many, his name was Legion.
The demons pleaded with Jesus
Not to send them into the deep;
So He sent them into a herd of swine
That fed on a hillside steep,
They ran into the lake and drowned
And the demonic man was healed;
He wanted to stay with Jesus
But couldn't—this was the deal;
He must go back to his house
And show the miracle Christ had done
So the people of that city
Would know Jesus was God's Son.
Now many of Satan's demons
Are trying to attack you each day
So keep your mind stayed on Christ
And chase them all away.

Reference: Luke 8:26-39

July 9

There was a market at Jerusalem
And next to it was a pool;
When an angel stirred the waters
The first in was healed—that's *"cool"*.
One man laid by the pool
Thirty eight years without cease,
Unable to get in the water
To be healed of his disease.
Jesus saw him lying there
And said take up your bed;
Even though it was the Sabbath,
The man did as Jesus said.
When the Jews found out that Jesus
Had healed this man, so lame,
They began to persecute Him
For they now knew He was to blame.
These Jews lived under the law
And did not know about grace;
Jesus healed the man on the right day
And surely at the right place!

Reference: John 5:2-16

July 10

Paul said he had been warned
　By his brothers of the house of Chloe
That there were contentions among them
And he said that shouldn't be so.
Some of you say, I am of Paul,
Yet, I did not die for you;
Others say they're of Apollos
Who can save no one—that's true;
Christ Jesus is *not* divided,
We all baptize in His name,
He is the *only one* who saves
That is the reason why He came.

Reference: 1 Corinthians 1:11-13

July 11

Joshua told the tribes of Israel
That in times before the flood,
Their fathers served other gods;
They were of Adam's blood.
God took Abraham who loved Him
And multiplied his seed,
Through Isaac, Jacob and others,
And He met their every need.
God brought them out of Egypt
Through the wilderness to the sea
And drowned Pharaoh's army
So His people could be free.
God led them across the Jordan
And put the Amorites in their hands,
So they could live the good life
There in the Promised Land.
Everyone must make a choice
Of just who their god will be,
Joshua said, for me and my house
We'll serve the Lord, and only He.

Reference: Joshua 24:1-15

July 12

When we were without Christ
We were aliens and strangers,
Without hope and without God,
In a world so full of dangers;
But scriptures say Christ is in us
And that we are in Him;
We should seek those words out
And read each one of them.
For they build up our confidence
And they verify the place,
That we have in Jesus Christ
Given us by His saving grace;
We were all just sinners
But in Ephesians two thirteen
It tells us we were drawn to God
By Christ's blood that made us clean.

Reference: Ephesians 2:12-13

July 13

When God adopted us
He made us His heirs
And opened up His treasury
So His riches we could share.
This new abundant life
That God gives to you and me
Cannot be opened by anyone else
Only Jesus has the key.
We are brothers and sisters
In Christ who set us free
And rich in His blessings
That He shares abundantly.

Reference: Romans 8:15-17

July 14

Adam and Eve in that garden
Really did have it made
Then they did something stupid;
The one thing God forbade.
There were other trees in the garden
That bore delicious fruit
But they ate of the forbidden one,
The others did not suit.
These two lusted for that tree
And their thinking was not sound;
The apple in the tree didn't mess things up
It was the *pair* down on the ground.
When we are tempted by Satan
To the point where we are hurting
We can defeat him with God's Word
Of this fact I am certain.

Reference: Genesis 2:8-17; 3:1-6

July 15

When you're in troubled waters
   Being tossed about by waves,
You'll show your true colors
By the way that you behave;
Just remember God is with you
And maintain faith and confidence;
Be courageous and not fearful
And Christ will come to your defense.
Keep your eyes fixed on Christ
And He will keep you afloat,
He'll reach out His strong hand
And He'll stabilize your boat.

Reference: Matthew 14:24-32

July 16

David just had a slingshot
When he faced that big guy
But knew he would kill Goliath,
This is the reason why.
God had helped him save his sheep
When he killed a lion and a bear;
He knew when he faced Goliath,
His Lord would be right there.
In this life we all face troubles,
Some are small, and some are giants
But if we trust God like David did,
We, like him, can be defiant!

Reference: 1 Samuel 17:32-51

July 17

The hungry lions in that den
  Had not been fed for days
So when Daniel was tossed in
They should have eaten him in a rage.
But God was there with him
And He shut those lions' jaws;
He knew Daniel loved Him
For he always kept His laws.
God did this miracle for Daniel
And He'll do one just for us
If we will love and trust Him
And believe in His Son Jesus.

Reference: Daniel 6:16-22

July 18

Adam and Eve sinned in the Garden
When they ate of that tree,
It wasn't as if they didn't know,
They did it deliberately.
David took another man's wife
Then had her husband slain,
He was a man after God's own heart
But did something God disdained.
Jonah didn't obey God
He just turned and ran
But didn't get away from God,
There is not a man who can.
Noah found grace in God's eyes
And built that great big ark,
Yet later got drunk with wine
And things looked mighty dark.
When Moses struck the rock
Water came out, and there were cheers
But this angered God so much,
That eleven day trip took forty years.
All these men loved their God,
Yet, everyone got out of line
But each asked for forgiveness
And everything turned out fine.

July 19

The Book of Solomon is all about
The intimacy of married bliss
And is a good example that
Our love of God should be like this.
It is a picture of the Bridegroom,
And His lovely Bride the Church,
Whom Christ loves so dearly;
If only we could love that much.
It is also a picture of Israel
As God's betrothed Bride
And like Israel we're His children
And He's always by our side.

Reference: Songs of Solomon

July 20

Paul wrote some of his epistles,
From dark, damp prison cells,
Not from sunny beach resorts
Where things were going well;
As Saul, he caused much suffering
And agony, grief and pain,
But once he met Christ Jesus
From all malice he abstained.
He went from a persecutor
To a preacher of much fame,
There on the road to Damascus
When his life was changed;
We may never be as bad as Paul
But may feel we're even worse,
Yet, God will forgive each of us
And take away old Satan's curse.

Reference: Book of Romans

July 21

God looked down from above
And saw the wickedness on earth.
He decided to destroy everything
But He saved Noah, a man of worth.
God told him to build an ark
And flood waters would then rise
But they'd be safe inside the ark
From rain falling from the skies;
When the waters finally subsided
God sent a promise in a rainbow,
That this would never happen again
And that's a good thing to know.
As God looks on this earth today
Do you think that He might see
Some of Noah's good in us
And save someone through you and me?

Reference: Genesis 6:5 thru 9:9-16

July 22

Joseph's brother's hated him,
   He was a little tattletale;
They knew Jacob loved him more,
It was as *clear as a bell*.
Joseph was born in Jacob's old age
And on him his father did dote.
His brothers hated him even more
When he wore that colorful coat;
This brought out the worse in them
And they came up with a scheme
To get rid of this boastful lad
Who told them his prideful dream.
This story surely proves to us
How God turns the bad around,
He re-united these brothers
And great love did then abound.

Reference: Genesis 37:2-19; 45:1-14

July 23

All the people came to Solomon
To hear the wisdom in his heart
And his awesome judgments
That all were so very smart;
But then he disobeyed God
Doing what God hated so,
He loved many strange women,
Even the daughter of a Pharaoh;
He had seven hundred wives
And they turned his heart away
From God to their own idols,
That he worshipped every day.
God had warned him of this
But Solomon did it anyhow
And God would have to punish him
But at some later date, not now;
Solomon brought this on himself
Because he compromised,
That's how Satan attacks us today,
It's an old trick that he devised.
So when he puts it in your mind
To do something you know is wrong,
Say," *Get thee behind me Satan*"
And let your faith be strong.

Reference: *1 Kings 10:24-29; 11:1-9*

July 24

In God's Word Paul tells us
To this world don't be conformed
But by the love and blood of Jesus,
To His pure nature be transformed.
When we accept Him as our Lord
There is a renewing of our mind,
That we may prove the will of God,
That's perfect, acceptable, good and kind.

Reference: Romans 12:2

July 25

The strong should bear the infirmities
Of the weak for it is written,
Even Christ didn't please Himself
But for others He was smitten.
Let's not just please ourselves
But try hard to please our neighbor.
In so doing we'll please God
And win His grateful favor.

Reference: Romans 15:1-3

July 26

Christians are left here to serve others;
To help neighbors we may see,
Who have a very special need
That could be filled by you or me.
Any and everything we do
Should be done in God's name,
That He may be glorified
And not done for self fame.
Jesus served his people
He went about doing good.
All Christians will do likewise
If they mimic Him like they should.

July 27

When we pray for something
    And then think God's too slow,
We must just rest in the Lord,
God could be saying no.
Also know He may say yes,
Or He may say wait a while,
He may want us to sit back
And trust Him like a child.
When we ask God to fill our needs
Sometimes we need to be still;
He will do it in His own time
If what we want is in His will.

Reference: Psalms 37:7

July 28

Let me tell you about Lillian
My much loved Christian aunt
Who always witnessed for Jesus,
So very bold—without restraint;
I was very uneasy around her,
Something inside troubled me,
When she talked about the blood
That Christ shed at Calvary.
I lived a pretty decent life
And thought I was a good man,
I even taught a Sunday school class
So I did not understand.
I thought she was a fanatic
But there was no hypocrisy,
She wanted me to know Jesus
And finally got through to me;
I then considered myself worse
Than a drug addict or a thief;
I had been just a hypocrite,
I only had a false belief.
Lillian is now in Heaven
Where someday I'll be too
For she told me all about Jesus,
Like I'm now telling you.

July 29

Jeremiah says his God is true
 And His words shall ever remain,
Yet, those who worship idols
Put forth their faith in vain.
They go out and cut down trees
And deck them with silver and gold,
Which they fasten using nails
And then watch their shapes unfold.
They stand upright like a palm tree
But cannot breathe or speak
And can't move but must be carried
By men who are strong, not weak.
These idols could do no evil
And this seems very queer,
They also could do no good,
Yet, they caused a lot of fear.
This man of God sure knew
His God was a God of might,
The only living true God
And scripture proves him right.
Let us not worship false gods
That can come in many forms
But worship only God and Jesus
And our lives will be transformed.

Reference: Jeremiah 10:1-15

July 30

We seem to picture Satan with horns,
Wearing a cape of black and red
And having a pointed goatee
But we are being misled.
He goes about to and fro
On earth just oozing charm
And before we recognize him
We'll be done much harm.
He's the one who always says
It won't hurt to take one drink
But that one leads to another
And we have been hoodwinked.
Satan has many disguises
And he adapts to many styles
All of which are tempting
And by which we are beguiled.
There are times when we invite him,
To come in, and I beg your pardon,
When we would have kicked him out,
If he looked like that snake in the garden!

July 31

Satan will trick and mislead,
Fill our lives with evil deeds,

Give us falsehoods to believe,
Knowing we will be deceived.

He will also steal our joy,
And our character he'll destroy,

He'll make us sin, which is his ploy,
While all the time being very coy.

This is the truth we've now heard,
Not to believe would be absurd,

To defeat Satan, that old bird,
Just stay daily in God's Word!

August

August 1

God uses all kinds of people
Just like He used Rahab,
The harlot at the wall of Jericho,
Who kept the spies from getting nabbed;
She protected these two men,
Even though she had to lie
And God saved her whole family;
She believed in Him—that's why.
Some may be a type of Rahab,
Who you'd think God couldn't use
But if they believed in God like her,
They may be the first He'd choose.

Reference: Joshua 2:1-18

August 2

Word after word,
Line after line,
As we read God's Word
Or any other time,
We must strive to keep
His Holy Word intact
And not change its meaning
Or delete a fact.
God will be pleased
And we will be wise
If we'll keep His truth
And not compromise.
So don't even change
A jot or a tittle*
If it would alter God's Law
A lot or a little!

Reference: Matthew 5:18
*smallest letter

August 3

God sent His messenger before Jesus
To prepare for Him the way,
His name was John the Baptist,
He would baptize Christ one day.
People came from Judea
And from all Jerusalem
Confessing their sins to John
And being baptized by him;
He was that voice in the wilderness,
As written in the book of Isaiah,
Crying, prepare the way of the Lord,
Who would be the Jew's Messiah.
While John baptized with water,
Christ baptized with the Holy Ghost
And once we've accepted Jesus
We become the Spirit's permanent host.

Reference: Mark 1:1-8

August 4

We all know the story about Noah,
Who God told to build an ark;
He obeyed God and did it
But was completely "in the dark";
God watered the earth with dew
So Noah had never seen rain
And didn't know what that could be
But He never did complain.
God loved Noah and saved him
For being righteous, yes it's true,
And since we are Noah's descendants,
When He saved Noah He saved us too.
God continues to save mankind,
Yet, not from some big flood
But from his own sinful ways,
Through Jesus' righteous blood!

Reference: Genesis 6:8-22

August 5

When Bartimaeus heard Jesus,
He was as blind as he could be
But believed Christ was God's Son
And received his sight, you see.
Many people go through life
As they say *"blind as a bat"*,
But they are not really blind
They don't know where *it's* at.
What I'm trying to say is
Their eyes are open, but,
They do not know Christ as Lord;
It's like their eyes are glued shut.
Their eyesight must be restored
Like that of Bartimaeus
And that can only happen,
If they put their faith in Jesus!

Reference: Luke 18:35-43

August 6

Dear one in Christ don't ever forget
That Satan is a big liar
And he is very angry at you,
For you'll miss his lake of fire.
He'll try to make you think he's right
But he's a great big phony,
He will do everything he can
To ruin your Christian testimony;
So turn your back on Satan
That old devil of deceit;
Keep your eyes stayed on Christ
And you'll have Satan in full retreat.

Reference: John 8:44

August 7

This joke is about a woman
That a thief did accost;
She knew if he stole her purse
All her money would be lost.
She loudly shouted at him
Acts two thirty eight!
This surprised the thief
And caused him to hesitate;
He then dropped her purse
And turned around and ran,
A policeman caught him right away
But he did not understand.
He said, why did you drop her purse?
You'd outrun her with your gait;
He said, but she had an axe
And two thirty eights!
This woman knew her scripture;
She was saying to him, repent;
It worked out fine for her
For it saved her every cent.

Reference: Acts 2:38

August 8

Nebuchadnezzar had a vision
Of a tree so strong and tall,
It reached into the heavens
With fruit and meat for all;
When Daniel interpreted this dream
It really troubled him
For it favored the king's enemies,
It really would please them.
He said the tree is you, O King,
You have grown big and strong
But you have become prideful
And to God that is so wrong.
Your kingdom will be taken away,
You'll dwell with beasts of the field,
Until you learn it is God who rules
And gives kingdoms to those He will.
Daniel said break off your sins
By using God's righteousness
And by showing mercy to the poor
But this king could care less.
As he went into his palace
Bragging of his might and power,
There came a voice from heaven;
His kingdom was taken in that hour.
All the predictions came true,
Then the king lifted up his eyes
And praised and blessed the Lord
Because he finally realized,
God rules and does as He pleases
And no one can stay His hand,
Then God restored his kingdom
And added honor to this man.

Reference: Daniel 4:4-37

August 9

King Belshazzar held a feast
And his wives and concubines
Used vessels from the temple,
From which to drink their wine
And as the king praised his gods,
A man's fingers wrote on the wall;
His wise men were dumbfounded
So Daniel then was called.
He read the writing on the wall
And told Belshazzar what it meant,
He said your days are numbered,
Your years of ruling almost spent.
You've been weighed and found wanting,
(His reign was not "up to par"),
Your kingdom is given to your enemies
Who will rule better than you by far.
All this happened because Belshazzar
Worshiped gods of silver and gold
And that night this king was slain
Just like Daniel had foretold.
Are there other gods in your life,
Such as, people, things, or "mon"?
If so you must make a change
God must be your only one.

Reference: Daniel 5:1-30

August 10

One day Ruth went into the fields
Where men were gathering corn
And worked behind them all day long,
Although being tired and worn.
The fields belonged to Boaz,
Who was one of Naomi's kin
And he had heard about Ruth,
Who was Naomi's dearest friend.
He told his men when they reaped
To leave some stalks behind
For Ruth to glean in his fields;
Boaz was being so very kind.
He said come over and eat with me
And share some bread and wine;
She sat with him and his handmaids
And ate and had a good time.
There was now plenty of food
For Naomi and Ruth to eat;
God really blessed this woman
For being so kind and sweet.

Reference: Ruth 2

August 11

Samuel made his sons judges
Over Israel and its tribes;
They were dishonest in their ways
And unlike Samuel, they took bribes.
These people had rejected God
So when they cried out in grief,
God did not hear their cries
And He gave them no relief.
So the people asked him for a king
But Samuel told them he'd be mean,
He would make slaves of everyone
And much pain and misery bring.
They got the king they wanted
And because they made a fuss
God gave them what they deserved,
Let's don't let that happen to us.

Reference: 1 Samuel 8:1-22

August 12

God delivered His people Israel
To the Philistines for forty years
For they did evil in His eyes,
And had lost their reverent fears;
But one loyal man was Manoah
A man with a childless wife,
God had sent an angel to tell her
She'd conceive and give new life.
She must not drink strong drink
Or bring a razor to his head,
He'd bring Israel out of bondage
So she did just as he said.
Manoah burned a goat on the altar
And the angel went up in the flame
Then it happened as God promised
And their baby Samson came.
These two had kept their faith in God,
While living in a land so vile
And He blessed their faithfulness;
This son made it all worthwhile.

Reference: Judges 13:1-24

August 13

Boaz fell in love with Ruth
And he was ready to marry
But there was a closer kinsman
So for a while he had to tarry.
Boaz went to this kinsman
And these two men sat down
Along with the ten elders
That Boaz brought to town.
He said you are the closer kin
And have the right to claim her
But if you don't wish to do so,
I'll marry her and rename her.
So Boaz married Ruth
And she later bore him a son
He'd be the grandfather of David,
Who fought Goliath one on one.
He would be Naomi's grandson,
Whom she would help to raise
And he'd be a blessing to her
And she'd give God all the praise.
God not only provided for Naomi
But He also provided for Ruth;
He'll do that for all who trust Him,
This story is the living proof.

Reference: Ruth 4:1-18

August 14

Would you mourn for a dead enemy?
Like David did for Saul,
The man who tried to kill him
With a spear against a wall;
Who also tried to kill his son
Because he was David's friend
And helped him to escape,
Much to his father's chagrin;
But regardless of Saul's actions
David remained loyal and true
And forgave his beloved king;
What an example for me and you.

Reference: 2 Samuel 1:17-27

August 15

While flying over America
Way up high in the sky
Looking down on the countryside
It suddenly dawned on me that I,
Was seeing this beautiful land
Somewhat from God's viewpoint,
And I was overwhelmed that this
Is a country He did anoint.
I feel I had one advantage
I couldn't see all the sin,
I saw the rivers and streams
And the way they twist and bend,
I saw the mountains and the plains,
The rectangles, ovals and squares,
And couldn't see the hearts of men
Caught up in the devil's snares;
Yes, God has blessed America
And isn't it a crying shame,
That as much as He has done for us,
Some still profane His name!

August 16

Jonah was displeased with God
And his anger did abound
For God chose to save Nineveh,
Yes, all the people in that town.
God had love and compassion
But poor Jonah he had none,
He wanted God to destroy that city;
He would rejoice when it was done.
Jonah went to another place
Where God provided him shade
And he was very comfortable,
He really thought he had it made.
But God had others plans
And he sent a lowly worm
To eat the vine and Jonah got mad,
Then God said to him so firm,
Do you have a right to be angry
About that dead and withered vine?
If he had been concerned about Nineveh
Everything would be just fine.
God cares about every man
That's why Nineveh was saved
And Jonah was chosen to help Him,
Even though he misbehaved;
In this story about Jonah
God has made it very clear,
He does not want to lose one soul
For each one to Him is dear.

Reference: Jonah 4:1-11

August 17

God gave David great victories
No matter where he went,
For he did that which was right
And he had the Lord's consent.
He asked if any of Saul's kin remained
So he could go and make
A gesture of kindness toward them,
He would do this for Jonathan's sake.
Jonathan's son was the only one left
And he was crippled in both feet,
So David sent for this poor man
To make his gesture complete.
David then restored to him
The land of his grandfather Saul
And his grandfather's many cattle,
But wait!—that's not all.
He let Saul's servants farm his land,
They also harvested his crops
And he ate from the king's table
So to him King David was "tops".
David had searched and found this man
Instead of wondering or guessing,
And showed him God's awesome love
That came with many blessings.

Reference: 2 Samuel 9:1-13

August 18

Prayer is a very powerful tool
　That God wants us to use
To win all of our battles
Against the devil if we choose.
Never say, "All I can do is pray",
For that doesn't make much sense
We must not keep the best for last,
Prayer is our first line of defense.
Not only should we talk to God
When down on our knees praying
But we should also listen to Him
And take heed of what He's saying.

August 19

Do not keep the ones you love
Spinning on a potter's wheel,
Trying to mold and reshape them,
Just to change the way *you* feel.
You must accept them as they are
Because you won't have good results,
God is the Potter—that's His job,
Grow up, act like an adult.
Then they'll love and respect you
And when you, yourself, are down
They'll be there by your side
They'll be the first to come around.

August 20

Elisha did many miracles
For God gave power to him,
One time he saved a woman's son
And he caused an axe to swim.
Once he fed a hundred men
With a little corn and barley bread,
He also took spoiled pottage
And made it delicious instead,
He asked God to open a boy's eyes
When surrounded by evil forces
And then the boy saw around him,
God's chariots of fire, and many horses;
Yes, Elisha was a man of God
Whom God was quick to use
Blessing other people through him
For he never once refused.

Reference: Book of 2 Kings

August 21

Sometimes we get too busy
To talk to God each day
But we shouldn't let that happen,
We must take time to pray.
God loves each one of us
And wants us to commune,
So if you miss a daily prayer
You must start back real soon.
Yes, God really loves you
Don't fret, sit back, and relax,
His mercy and grace are with you
That is a given fact!

August 22

When David heard of the death of Saul
And that of Jonathan, he lamented,
He loved them both so very much,
His heart and soul was tormented.
David cried out, O Israel,
Glory lies slain on your heights
For there your king has fallen,
May God now condemn that site.
May the mountains of Gilboa
Where King Saul was slain
Never again have rain or dew
And never more yield grain.
Saul's shield was defiled there
And is no longer rubbed with oil,
Jonathan's bow never turned back
Nor Saul's sword return unspoiled.
These two were smarter than lions
And both as *tough as leather,*
They always fought side by side,
They even died together.
David grieved for both these men
But Jonathan was like a brother
And he had more grief for him,
Than for Saul or any other;
When you truly love someone
Even though they have perished
And are no longer with you,
Their memories will be cherished.

Reference: 2 Samuel 1:17-27

August 23

A woman was so destitute
And completely without hope,
Her creditors would take her sons;
She was "at the end of her rope".
So Elijah wanted to know
If she had anything for her toils
But she said all that she had,
Was just a single pot of oil.
He told her to borrow vessels,
To get many, not a few
And set aside the pot she had
Then he'd tell her what to do.
He said when you come back in
Just shut the door behind,
And pour your oil in the vessels,
Each and every one you find.
She then filled all those vessels
And sold some oil to pay her debts
There still was plenty of oil left,
And all her needs were met.
This woman had faith in God
And did exactly as Elijah said;
God blessed her through this prophet.
He'll bless us through Christ instead.

Reference: 2 Kings 4:1-7

August 24

The Holy Bible tells us
To let our light shine,
Now yours could be brighter,
Or not as bright as mine.
Your light may be a twenty five
Or a two hundred watt
But that doesn't really matter,
It's how you use what you've got.
A small bulb gives much light
In a room that's dark as pitch,
So you must not hesitate,
Just flip on your switch.
Then your little light will shine
To help light this world so dark
And it may help to save someone;
It may just be that needed spark!

Reference: Matthew 5:16

August 25

Sometimes we think we're in a groove
But we're really in a rut,
Like those you see on muddy roads
That your wheels get in, but,
They are so very deep
There's no way you can get out,
And no matter how hard you try
You need some help, no doubt;
So just put God in control
And then on Him rely,
He'll help you out of that rut
Into a groove that's nice and dry.

August 26

Amalek was the grandson of Esau,
The one who gave up his birthright,
He was a constant enemy of God
And God's people he did fight.
Moses told Joshua to go out
And do battle with Amalek
While he and Aaron and Hur,
Would help keep the fight in check;
Moses stood on a high hill
With a staff in his hand,
There was power when he held it up
And Joshua defeated every man,
But if Moses lowered the staff,
Which he did when he got tired,
The enemy then prevailed
And that wasn't what God desired.
Aaron and Hur found a rock
For Moses to sit down on
And helped hold up his staff,
So power flowed from God's throne.
Yes, Joshua defeated Amalek,
I am very happy to report,
He relied on Moses, Aaron and Hur,
But mostly on God's support,
There are times when we need help
Like Joshua got from those men
But our main support is God
And on Him we can depend.

Reference: Exodus 17:8-13

August 27

King Abijah died and was buried
And his son Asa reigned in his stead,
He did right in the eyes of God
And once cried out to Him and said,
Lord it is nothing for you
To help those without much power,
So help us O Lord our God.
(He needed Him in this hour.)
This enemy had a million men
And three hundred chariots,
But God smote them everyone
And they deserved what they got.
Asa tore down idols and images,
Even one built by the queen,
Who also was his mother
And that was a very good thing.
Yet, he didn't remove the "high places"
And he later did a great sin,
For he no longer relied on God
And that's what "done him in"!
Are there "high places" in your life?
Obstacles you need to remove,
Such as lack of trust in God
So you can stay in His groove?

Reference: 2 Chronicles 14:1-15; 15:16-17; 16:1-9

August 28

Yesterday was once today
And today was once tomorrow.
We're the result of our past lives
Sometimes that's to our sorrow.
Scripture says God is not mocked,
A man reaps what he sows,
But he will reap much more
And much later, that we know!
Whether you're a believer or not
This truth applies to everyone;
You'll be judged one day,
For the deeds you've done.
Whether you do good deeds or bad
That's something you must decide.
Just remember God knows your heart
And there's nothing you can hide.

Reference: Galatians 6:7-8

August 29

Why did God put up with Israel
Who at times made His anger hot?
And why does He put up with us,
Are we not of the same lot?
When He made them a promise,
They just needed to obey
And we like them so many times
Get sidetracked along the way.
God kept them out of the Promised Land
But finally let some inside,
Yet, He left their enemy there
To be *a thorn in their side!*
If God is to keep His promises
We must trust Him with all our heart
And do exactly what He tells us,
Then He'll surely do His part.

Reference: Judges 2:11-23

August 30

There are times when Satan
Always seems to hang around
And cause our circumstances
To trip us up or knock us down;
That's when we should be like Job
And not fuss at God, or curse
But continue to trust in Him
Or matters could get worse.
We can defeat the devil
If we'll just understand
We can't do it all alone
We need God's helping hand.

August 31

Set your mind on good and keep it set
For what you think is what you get,

You really need to gird your mind,
What you think returns in like kind.

Think good thoughts and on the morrow
You'll be happy, without sorrow.

Don't dwell on bad things, if you do
Satan can have his way with you.

If somehow Satan gets a hold
Stand up to him—be very bold.

This is a truth I know you've heard,
To defeat him quote God's Word!

September

September 1

We're like farmers of the field
Who go out and sow seed,
Then put their trust in God
To send the rain they need.
Yet, they don't sit idly by
They're attentive to their crops,
They till and plow the ground
And often weeds they chop.
Yes, we must do our part
And let God do the rest,
Then when *our* crop comes in
It will be the very best.
Be sure you sow good seed,
Not "wild oats" in each row,
For what you sow will follow you;
And you'll reap more than you sow!

Reference: Galatians 6:7-8

September 2

Once you have been born again
You need to seek God's heart
And be willing to serve Him
Then He will do His part.
He'll use you to spread His Word
To those around you who don't know
And you'll be His ambassadors
Everywhere you go.
Christ was made sin for us,
He who knew no sin,
That we be made righteous
And take the Gospel to all men.

Reference: 2 Corinthians 5:20-21

September 3

There are many cults today
Whose beliefs are fragmented;
The Bible says they are fools;
It says just what God intended.
They believe false doctrines
And lead many people astray,
From the truth in God's Word
That Jesus is the *only* way.
He is the truth and the life
And no man should ever bother,
To try to find another way
To get to God the Father!

Reference: John 14:6

September 4

Paul saw false gods in Athens
And one day he was shown,
An altar someone erected,
Inscribed to a god unknown;
Paul gave them a "shock treatment"
Like you'd do to a swimming pool,
He said, I worship the true God
Who has sovereign rule.
Paul preached to these people
And witnessed bold and brave
Telling them all about Jesus,
The only one who could save.
One of the truths He told them
While standing on Mars Hill,
Was they must believe in Christ
In order to be in God's Will.

Reference: Acts 17:22-34

September 5

There's a lady preacher on T.V.
That my wife and I admire,
Teaching God's Word in a way
That sets our hearts on fire.
She tells us how to enjoy life
By staying in God's will,
She never compromises His Word
And says it is relevant still.
Every word out of her mouth
Encourages us with hope and joy
She is truly a servant of God,
Yes, she's the "Real McCoy"!
Her main topic is Jesus,
So the seed of salvation is planted;
She tells you to accept Him today
You can't take another day for granted!

September 6

One day after healing a servant
Jesus went to a city called Nain,
As He neared the gate to the city
He met a long procession train;
A dead man was being carried out
The son of a widowed mother,
And he was her only son
She did not have another.
Jesus had compassion on her
And said to her don't weep,
He touched the open coffin
Of this son in death's sleep,
He said to the son arise
And he sat up and began to speak,
Christ then gave him to his mother
Don't you imagine she was *"freaked"*?
This woman was now so happy
And very grateful to Him,
Everyone there glorified God,
Knowing He had been with them.
When Christ does a great thing
In our lives, just for us,
We must always glorify God
And also our Lord Jesus!

Reference: Luke 7:11-16

September 7

The way to jump start your life
Each and every bless-ed day,
Is to wake up very early
And talk to God—yes, pray.
Turn everything over to Him,
Let Him work through you,
Keep self in the background
And He'll bless everything you do.
You'll feel His power and glory
And His loving kindness too,
As you praise Him with your lips
Great joy will come to you.

September 8

P aul knew he would benefit
Whether he lived or died;
Alive he would live for Christ,
If dead, lose the thorn in his side.
He'd be in Heaven with Jesus
With no more sickness or pain,
No more beatings or jail time,
This would all be for his gain.
He'd be in no more shipwrecks
And have no more snake bites,
There'd be no more persecutions,
This much to his delight!
Paul went though much misery
But always went that extra mile
And he loved Christ so much,
It made his suffering all worthwhile.

Reference: Philippians 1:21; Book of Acts, various verses

September 9

Once saved, always saved,
The Bible makes that clear
But Satan will surely tempt you,
He'll give you the false idea,
That you can do all the things
You did before, that weren't right;
He does this by putting them
Squarely in your sight.
You won't lose your *relationship*
With God if you do roam
But if you lose your testimony,
He may decide to take you home.
Your *fellowship* with God
Is the main thing that you'd lose
So when you're tempted by Satan
Be very careful what you choose.

Reference: Hebrews 9:28

September 10

God has shown you, O man,
That which is right and good
And what He requires of you,
(I hope that's understood).
He wants you to be just,
And show love and mercy,
To walk humbly with Him
And be His companion, you see.
Your close fellowship with God
Is what *it* is all about
And for every Christian,
Something they can't do without.

Reference: Micah 6:8

September 11

James and John came to Jesus,
(These two sons of Zebedee),
Asking for a special place
With Him in Eternity,
They wanted to sit beside Him
So His glory they could share;
Jesus said that would be given
To them for whom it was prepared;
What they asked Him to do
Was not His right to give,
The other disciples heard them
And it pierced them like a shiv.
Whoever would be greatest
Shall be a servant to all,
This is what Christ said to them
And says to us who heed God's call.

Reference: Mark 10:35-44

September 12

Our eternal life depends
On a question in Matthew
That Jesus asked the Pharisees,
Found in chapter twenty two.
What think ye of Christ
And whose son is He?
Son of David was the answer,
Given by these Pharisees;
Christ asked then how could David
In the Spirit call Him Lord?
Christ couldn't be David's son.
(He couldn't even be his Ward).
The Pharisees did not know
Christ was God's Son, or the fact,
That if you believed in Him
Your Salvation was intact.

Reference: Matthew 22:41-45

September 13

Mark says Jesus came
Not to be ministered to
But to minister to others
And that included me and you.
Now if our Lord Himself
Served mankind in this way
We must follow in His footsteps
And serve others everyday.
Christ not only served on earth
But serves in eternity
Where He still makes it possible
For all sinners to be free!

Reference: Mark 10:45

September 14

My God shall supply your needs
According to His riches in glory
And He will do it through Jesus,
It's the truth, not just some story.
We should be more like Paul
Whose trust in God was sound;
We need to be able to suffer
And be able to abound.
We must keep our faith in God
During the good times and the dire,
Looking for Him to meet our needs
And fulfill our least desire.

Reference: Philippians 4:18-19

September 15

God gave Moses an order
When up on Mount Sinai,
To tell all of His people
They would see Him by and by.
They would be a kingdom of priests,
Was Moses' declaration,
And a peculiar treasure of God,
They would be His Holy nation.
They couldn't come on the mountain
Or even its borders touch,
If they did so they would die,
Moses told them all this much.
First they washed their clothes
And on the third day they assembled,
Then lightning and thunder came
Like a trumpet, and they trembled!
God gave the Ten Commandments
And told the people to make an altar;
They did just as He commanded
And not one person faltered.
God gave more instructions,
Which His people heard that day;
God blessed His people mightily
For they heeded and obeyed!

Reference: Exodus 19:3 thru 24:3

September 16

If you seem to have a record
  Spinning around and around,
Inside your head it's Satan
Just trying to get you down;
He surely wants to keep you
In that old proverbial rut
Of thinking negative thoughts
But you can hit him in his gut.
Don't dwell on that bad stuff
That he puts inside your head
But brighten up your day,
Thinking just good thoughts instead!

September 17

Jesus is God's sin bearer,
   Who bears and hides all guilt
So His Father never sees our sin,
His blood covers it like a quilt.
The Bible says *all* have sinned
And God's standards have not met,
Except those who know Jesus,
And their sin God does forget.
Yes, everyone needs Jesus
God's Son who died for sin;
He's the way we get to Heaven,
He's our Savior and friend.

Reference: Hebrews 9:28; Romans 3:23

September 18

You can be sure and certain
What you hope for will come true,
If you've received a promise from God
He will do it just for you.
These are words of wisdom
I heard a Bible teacher say,
Who led many people to Jesus
Because she walked in His ways;
She believed God's promise,
If she sowed the Gospel seed
He would water and nurture it
So those who heard it would believe.

September 19

To develop a relationship with God
You must know this is true,
That only God can forgive your sin
And He did it through Christ for you.
God adopted you as His child
When Christ died in your place,
For the sin that separated you
From God's love and grace.
Christ too, was separated from God,
Not due to any sin of His;
When He hung on that cross
He was taking care of **our** "biz".
Don't miss God's fellowship,
Walk in His ways—always,
And He will stay close to you
The remainder of your days.

September 20

Timothy's mother was a Christian
And his father was a Greek;
Timothy believed like his mother
And her wisdom he did seek.
He was well spoken of
By people in other places
Because he always served God
And he stayed within His traces.
God used Timothy mightily
Along with His servant Paul
Because he spoke out for Jesus
Without any shame at all;
Timothy's mother rocked his cradle
And was the one who ruled his world;
Mom, you should be just like her
When teaching your boy or girl.

Reference: Acts 16:1-4

September 21

The people you hang out with
Will determine who you'll be like;
It starts out very slowly
Like a small crack in a dike;
That little crack will cause that dam
To break and cause a flood,
With havoc and destruction
And debris and rocks and mud!
You life could end up like that
If you hang with the wrong crowd,
Or with just one wrong person
But you can make God proud;
Seek friends who are Christians
For they'll enhance your life,
They'll stick by you in troubles
And help ease your pain and strife.

September 22

Elijah challenged Baal's prophets,
All four hundred fifty of them
To bring fire down from heaven,
Yet, there was only one of him.
He asked the people how long
They would have divided opinions?
If the Lord be God, follow Him,
But if Baal; give him dominion.
The prophets called on Baal
From morning until noon,
Then Elijah mocked them,
Was he doing this too soon?
Elijah then called on His God
And God showed His great power,
For His fire consumed the altar
And even the stones that very hour.
When the people saw this
They each fell on their face
And said the Lord, He is God
And He bestowed on them His grace.

Reference: 1 Kings 18:19-39

September 23

There is but one true God
And between Him and men
There is one mediator
Who died for all men's sin!
Christ is that mediator
Who gave Himself for all,
Shedding His blood on the cross,
So all Christians can walk tall.
God loves each and every man
And wants them to believe
The truth that's in His Holy Word
So no one will be deceived.

Reference: 1 Timothy 2:5-6

September 24

On the day of Pentecost
The Apostles were in one accord,
When a mighty, rushing wind came
And filled the house and left no void.
There appeared cloven tongues
Like they were made of fire,
That sat down on each of them;
Their need for this was dire.
They were filled with the Spirit
That is, the Holy Ghost,
And began to speak in tongues,
Confusing the multitude, the host;
The people thought the Apostles
Were all drunk with wine
But Peter said the hour is early,
They are sober, they are fine.
Peter said men of Judea
God is loosing His Spirit someday,
Then whoever calls on Christ's name,
God will save him that way.
That's how it is in our time,
As prophesied by Peter,
Call upon the name of Jesus
And in Heaven He'll be your greeter.

Reference: Acts 2:1-21

September 25

Now the foolishness of God,
Is not foolish you understand
But is surely so much wiser
Than the greatest wisdom of man;
The weakness of God is stronger
Than the strongest of all men,
Keep this in your mind
For an explanation now begins.
God has chosen the foolish things
Of this wicked, sinful world
To confuse the so-called wise men
And their lack of knowledge unfurl.
God has chosen the weak things
To confound the things of might
And things which are despised,
And things that are not right.
Flesh itself should not glory
In the *presence* of the Lord
But should glory *in the Lord*
Like it says in His Holy Word.

Reference 1 Corinthians 1:25-31

September 26

The disciples became so busy
The widows were neglected
And the people came against them,
This should have been expected.
They felt the disciples didn't care
And that the widows were forsaken
But this was far from the truth,
These people were mistaken.
The disciples were busy preaching
And couldn't serve the widows' table,
So they picked seven men
And gave them a name; a label.
They would serve the widows
And be to them a shining beacon,
The disciples would preach the Gospel;
The seven would be their deacons.
We need to be like those men
Serving others while preachers, preach,
Then they will then have more time
For many other souls to reach.

Reference: Acts 6:1-7

September 27

Abraham was a righteous man
Who loved God very much
But He did something wrong
That put him out of touch.
He lied to King Abimelech
Saying Sarah was his sister
And the king took her as his wife
But never touched or kissed her.
God came to Abimelech
And said in a dream one night,
Sarah is another man's wife
And to touch her is not right.
Then Abraham told Abimelech
Sarah is my sister, indeed,
She's the daughter of my father,
This fact he did concede
But she's not my mother's daughter,
Is what he also told this king
But not saying she was his wife,
Was a very deceiving thing.
Abraham then prayed to God
And King Abimelech was healed,
The wombs of his wife and maidens
Were all opened—yes, unsealed.
Abraham found out the hard way,
As we may also by and by,
That telling someone a half-truth,
Is the same as telling a lie.

Reference: Genesis 20:2-18

September 28

Lord, you know I'm not an in-law
But I'm truly your blood kin,
Related to you through Jesus
Whose blood washed away my sin;
Your Word says I am in Christ
And that He is in me,
That You, Christ and the Spirit
Make up the Bless-ed Trinity.
When I accepted Jesus Christ
Your one and only Son,
I actually became a part of
The Holy three-in-one!
Before that I was an outlaw,
A criminal so notorious,
Breaking many of your laws
But now through Christ I'm glorious.
Thank you Lord for adopting me
With your unconditional love
Making me your beloved child,
Someday to dwell with you above.

September 29

When the disciples appointed deacons
Stephen was the first one chosen,
His heart was on fire for Christ,
Not lukewarm, cold or frozen.
Six other men were named,
So altogether there were seven,
The disciples laid hands on them,
Then prayed to God in Heaven;
These deacons ministered daily
And the Word of God increased
The number of disciples multiplied,
Don't you know God was pleased!
Is God also pleased with you
As your service to Him you give?
Do you help by serving others
As your life for Christ you live?

Reference: Acts 6:5-7

September 30

They gave a feast when Isaac was weaned
And Sarah saw something shocking!
Ishmael, the son of Hagar
Was watching and was mocking.
So Sarah told Abraham
To cast out Hagar and her son,
Abraham didn't want to do it
But God said it must be done.
He gave them bread and water
And into the wilderness they departed,
Yet, Abraham loved that son
And he was really broken hearted.
God had made a promise
To make Ishmael a great nation,
So when they ran out of water
It created a fearful situation.
Hagar lifted her voice to God
And cried out to Him, yes wept,
Then God provided water for her
And said His promise would be kept.
While there in the wilderness
Hagar felt so all alone,
But when she prayed to God
He made His presence known.
There may come a wilderness
In our lives either great or small
And we too must cry out to God
Then trust in Him, that's all.

Reference: Genesis 21:8-20

October

October 1

God will be a refuge
For all who are oppressed,
Who in times of trouble
Are weary and depressed,
He is much mightier
Than breakers of the sea;
He'll keep us in His hands
Safe from our enemy;
He says those who know Him
Will give Him all their trust
And He will not forsake them
For He is loving, kind and just;
Yes, God will stick by us
Through both thick and thin
And as we fight our battles
He's on our side, we'll win!

Reference: Psalms 9:9-10; 93:4

October 2

If you go through life
Investing only in stocks and bonds,
Relying on your brokers,
The Joes, the Jacks, the Johns.
They may increase your worth
And you may live in style,
You may feel secure
And yet all the while,
Deep down in your heart
Is a feeling you can't shake,
That you shouldn't live just for self
But also live for others sake.
You must share the Gospel,
The best investment in eternity,
One that will last forever
For the souls you help set free.

Reference: James 5:20

October 3

Stephen was so full of faith
He was God's spiritual tower,
He did miracles and wonders
And did them with God's power;
When some began to dispute him
He kept on preaching and never paused,
So a man bore false witness
And said he spoke against God's laws.
When Stephen said he saw Christ
On God's right hand they groaned
And cast him out of the city,
To the place where he'd be stoned;
He asked God to receive his spirit
And not lay this to their charge,
This was Stephen's last prayer
As he was hit with stones so large.
Stephen kept his faith in God
And became God's first martyr
And he wisely trusted in Him
No man could be smarter.

Reference: Acts 6:8-15; 7:56-60

October 4

God was so angry with His people
Destroying them was His intent
But Moses actually chided God
And caused Him to repent,
But first God said to Moses,
I am mad! Leave me alone;
The people had made an idol
And maybe put it on a throne.
God wanted to vent His wrath
And these people to consume
But when Moses intervened
It saved them all from doom.
Maybe it's okay for us
To get angry now and then
But if we don't repent
That anger becomes a sin.

Reference: Exodus 32:7-14

October 5

Are you a Good Samaritan?
Or just a prideful priest,
Maybe you're a Levite
Doing nothing—not the least;
God says you're a good neighbor
If you do all you can
To help someone in need
And give them a helping hand.
Would you go out of your way?
Spending your money and time
Or just turn and look away
Now that would be a crime.
There will be those times when,
The Golden Rule comes into play,
That's when we must treat others
In a very special way;
If we all did unto others
As we'd have them do unto us
This world would be a better place;
That rule works—it really does!

Reference: Luke 10:30-37

October 6

Life on this earth is a journey
And each of us is homeward bound,
Whether that home is up above
Or down beneath the ground.
As we live our lives each day,
I say this without hesitation,
We'll enjoy our journey more
If we know our final destination;
God has given us a map
Showing the only route to Heaven,
In Romans five, verse eight and nine
And partly in one through seven,
It tells us Jesus died for us,
That by His blood we're justified
And if we accept Him as Lord,
Our Salvation is verified.

Reference: Romans 5:1-9

October 7

God says a man is a sluggard
If he doesn't do his best
To provide for his family,
That is something God detests.
You can use your time
Most any way you choose
But every minute that you waste
Is valuable time you lose!
You can never get it back
No matter how hard you try,
It's a precious commodity
That money cannot buy.
Please use your time wisely
For all time is heaven sent,
Take good care of your family
And your time will be well spent.

Reference: Proverbs 6:6-9

October 8

What are you doing, for Heaven's sake!
Now that you've been saved;
Are you a witness for Jesus?
In the way that you behave;
Are you telling others about Him
And being a good role model,
Have you forsaken former sins?
Not keeping them to coddle.
Have you led someone to Jesus,
Saving them from Satan's fiery lake,
Again I ask you the question,
What are you doing, for Heaven's sake?

October 9

God created the heavens and earth
And all the creatures and man,
He did it for His own pleasure
And with His own two hands.
He enjoyed His creations,
They even made Him smile,
Till Eve sinned in the Garden
And became a disobedient child;
Then when Adam ate the apple
He also was to blame
And broke his fellowship with God
And it's a crying shame,
For if they hadn't done that
But had pleased God and obeyed,
There would still be a Garden of Eden
And today we'd have it made!

Reference: Genesis chapters 1 thru 3

October 10

Solomon asked God for wisdom,
Not riches of silver and gold.
He was much loved by God,
This is what we've been told.
He could have had anything
For which his heart yearned
But wisdom to rule his people
Was his biggest concern.
We too, must not be selfish
When we go to God in prayer
But should ask Him for wisdom
And like Solomon we must share.

Reference: 1 Kings 3:5-13

October 11

No one could find fault in Paul,
Not Felix, Festus or even Agrippa;
He came with pomp with Bernice,
Who may have worn a silver slipper.
Paul was to be sent to Jerusalem
But he did boldly refuse
And he appealed to Caesar,
He didn't want to face the Jews.
Agrippa listened to Paul's pleas
As he spoke in his own defense
And he was almost persuaded
For what Paul said made sense.
When we tell folks about Jesus
Let's do it with Paul's persuasion,
So they'll claim Him as Savior
And that will be a joyous occasion!

Reference: Acts 24, 25, 26

October 12

Chapter seventeen of Leviticus
Tells us life is in the blood
And it was sprinkled on the altar
To atone for sin, that's understood.
It goes way back to Eden
Where, Adam, the first man sinned
And it was passed on to us,
Very much to our chagrin;
Now Jesus' blood was perfect,
It was completely sin free,
So when He shed it on the cross
It atoned for *all* our sin, you see.

Reference: Leviticus 17:11

October 13

O Lord, when you made man
 And gave him his free will,
He gave in to Satan's ways
And he continues in them still.
Satan had the upper hand
And tempted man much more
But you leveled the playing field
And sent Christ to even the score;
Man still gives in to Satan
Much more than he oughta
But he can win by calling on Christ,
Even in the very last quarter!

October 14

Balaam woke up one morning,
Got on his donkey and went hence,
He knew God didn't want him to,
But he wasn't fully convinced.
God's anger was kindled toward him
And He put an angel in his way
But when the donkey turned aside,
Balaam smote her and she brayed.
The donkey saw the angel again
And thrust herself against the wall,
The force crushed Balaam's foot,
His heel, his toes, and all;
When he smote the donkey again
God opened the mouth of the ass
And it said, what have I done to you
To make these beatings come to pass?
Yes, God used a lowly donkey
To put His prophet back on track
And this time he listened to God,
So should we, and that's a fact.

Reference: Numbers 22:21-32

October 15

God called out to Moses
And spoke to him and said,
A man must bring a burnt offering
And put his hand upon its head,
It must be without blemish,
He must bring it on his own
To the door of the Tabernacle
For his sins to be atoned;
It would be cut into pieces,
Using a knife or a sword
And it will be a burnt sacrifice
Of sweet savor to the Lord;
Christ, the lamb without blemish,
Offered Himself without a fuss,
He was a sweet savor to God
And was the sacrifice for us.

Reference: Leviticus 1:1-9

October 16

There could be a good reason
The desires of your heart are lacking,
Maybe instead of trusting God
Your faith is back-tracking.
If you can identify the reason
And then that reason tame,
God will fulfill your desires
And things will never be the same.
Be specific in your request
And trust God to supply it;
If it's what's right for you
He will surely not deny it.

Reference: Psalms 37:3-4

October 17

Lord you created the universe
And hung the earth in space
The sun, the moon, the stars
You carefully put in place.
Then you decided to make man
And a smile came on your face,
You let him have dominion
And protected him with your grace
But he disobeyed you, Lord,
And broke a law you gave him,
When he sinned in the Garden,
Eating fruit from that tree limb;
We know we're insignificant
When you consider the universe,
Yet, you continue to love us
Though our actions still get worse;
Thank you God for making man
Whose light burns very dim,
When compared to that of Jesus
And for being mindful of him!

Reference: Genesis 1:1; Psalms 8:3-4

October 18

Shadrack, Meshack and Abednego
Were thrown in a furnace hot,
They were told to worship idols
But these God loving men would not!
They knew God could save them
And they made that very clear
But if He chose not to do so
They'd still trust and have no fear.
God did save these three men,
Scorched and singed they were not
But the flames killed the servants
Who threw them in that fire so hot!
O the faith of these three men,
In such a fearful situation,
They trusted God so completely
He saved them from devastation.
If we could have the faith
Of even the man Abednego,
We would be great witnesses
And very pleasing to God, I know.

Reference: Daniel 3:10-26

October 19

This is the day the Lord has made,
Keep this thought as you begin it
And as you do your daily chores,
Rejoice! And be glad in it.
The Lord is there by your side,
Face your day without fear
For what can man do to you?
As long as God is near.

Reference: Psalms 118:6-24

October 20

Paul was the greatest apostle,
His witness never ceased,
Yet, he was very humble
And said he was the least.
As he preached about Jesus
Paul certainly understood
Of all his thoughts and deeds,
Not a one was all that good.
When compared to Jesus
His deeds were as filthy rags
And though he gave it his *"best shot"*
There was nothing on which to brag.
We must realize also
Whether our deeds are big or small,
They are a bunch of filthy rags
Like those of the Apostle Paul.

Reference: Ephesians 3:7-8; Isaiah 64:6

October 21

God made the lowly sparrow
He kept his eyes on it, no doubt,
And stayed right there with it
When its light of life went out;
If God cared for that sparrow
Watching over it till its death,
He surely cares much more for us;
He gave us life with His own breath.
You know what that song says,
And I most certainly agree,
"If his eye is on the sparrow,
Then I know He watches me".

Reference: Matthew 10:29-31

October 22

Give and it will be given to you,
To some that may sound funny
But that verse speaks of many things
And not just giving money.
Giving a little of your time
To help someone in need,
Is sometimes more helpful
Than giving money—indeed;
Also giving of your love,
Is something you should learn,
That will bring joy to others
And you'll reap joy in return.

Reference: Luke 6:38

October 23

We know those who follow Jesus
Have a great battle to fight
It is spiritual in nature
Against what is wrong and right.
Even though we walk in the flesh
We do not battle with it,
Our warfare is against Satan
Who gives all Christians "fits"!
Cast down vain imaginations
In order to loosen his stronghold
And bring our thoughts into captivity
Then speak out for Christ real bold.

Reference: 2 Corinthians 10:3-5

October 24

As Jesus came off mountain
Followed by a great multitude,
A leper came and worshipped Him,
That had a believing attitude
And said Lord if you want to
You can make my body heal
And Jesus put forth His hand
And said to him, I will.
That leper had much faith
And knew Jesus was no phony,
So now instead of being a leper
He became a living testimony.
Now you are not a leper
But this is a given fact,
You can be a living testimony,
For Christ in the way you act.

Reference: Matthew 8:1-4

October 25

When Jesus went to Peter's house,
　　Peter's mother-in-law had a fever
But as Jesus touched her hand,
The sickness seemed to leave her.
She got out of her sick bed
And ministered unto them,
Then He healed many others
That they brought to Him.
The love and power of Jesus
Followed Him wherever He went;
If we let His love work through us,
Others will think we're Heaven-sent.

Reference: Matthew 8:14-16

October 26

Paul had a "thorn in his flesh"
And it caused him lots of pain
But he kept on praising God
And never did complain.
We know he sought the Lord,
Not just once, but thrice
For Him to remove the thorn,
But God must have said, "No dice".
We'd like to know what his thorn was
But God says that's not our "biz",
We'd just compare ourselves to Paul
And say our thorn's worse than his.
Now if you have a "thorn in your flesh"
Whether it be sickness or pain,
If you handle it like Paul did,
God will make it for your gain.

Reference: 2 Corinthians 12:7-9

October 27

Jesus was filled with compassion;
 People were like sheep without a shepherd,
They were diseased and scattered
And needed to hear God's Word;
Christ said the harvest is plentiful
But the laborers they are few;
When He said pray for laborers
He was speaking of me and you.
We must be alert and ready
And always willing to share
The powerful Word of the Gospel
With the unsaved everywhere!

Reference: Matthew 9:36-38

October 28

A woman had just one farthing
Which we call the Widow's Mite,
It was just a lowly sum,
Yet, her heart was right.
What she dropped in the plate,
Was every cent she had,
Worth more than the other offerings,
For she did it with a heart so glad;
It's not just how much we give
But it's also our attitude
And whether it's a lot or a little,
We should give it with gratitude.

Reference: Mark 12:41-44

October 29

Blessed are they who fear God
And walk ever in His ways,
They'll eat the fruit of their hands
And be happy all their days.
A man's wife will be fruitful
And with children he'll be blessed,
His children will honor him
And will help to give him rest.
This is God's promise to those
Who have reverence, and fear
And who walk in His ways;
He makes that promise clear.

Reference: Psalms 128

October 30

Beware of pride and jealousy
For they will bring you down,
Just like they did for King Saul
In First Samuel where it's found,
That he was very happy
When his people gave him praise
But when they lauded David
It filled his heart with rage.
Saul then tried to kill him
By spearing him against the wall
And that was the beginning
Of this great king's downfall;
People said Saul killed thousands
But if you multiplied that times ten,
It would be the number David killed
And that's what caused Saul to sin.
Don't be prideful like King Saul
But have a humble heart
And trust in God as David did;
That's the place we need to start.

Reference: 1 Samuel 18:6-11

October 31

Saul chased David everywhere
And tried to kill him many times
But David's chances to kill Saul
Were many more and were so prime.
David once cut Saul's robe
And showed a piece to the King,
Because he wanted him to know
He wouldn't do that evil thing.
Once Saul came into David's cave
And was sleeping very sound,
David took Saul's spear and jug
But did not *"put him down"*!
God gave Saul to the enemy
And Saul knew defeat was near
But didn't want to be captured
So he fell on his own spear.
David should have hated Saul,
Yet, forgave him time and again,
If we could forgive like David
We'd fit right in God's plan.

Reference: 1 Samuel 24:4-11; 31:1-7

November

November 1

Jeremiah went to the potter's house,
  Doing just as God told him
But the vessel on the wheel
Was marred from base to rim;
The potter began to remold it
And changed its entire shape,
Making it so very beautiful,
It would cause a man to gape.
God said He would do the same
To all the children of Israel,
Making them a new vessel
In which their spirit would dwell.
When we accept Jesus as Lord,
Whose Father is God the Potter;
At first we might not want to change
But sooner or later we just "gotta".

Reference: Jeremiah 18:1-6

November 2

We know Jesus is the vine
And the branches are you and I
But are we just sucker branches,
Causing the tree to die?
Sucker branches use much sap,
Yet, all of it is wasted,
They quickly grow very tall
But bear no fruit to be tasted.
Let us not be sucker branches
But let us be healthy and strong
And grow up quickly in the Word
And bear much fruit before long.

Reference: John 15:1-5

November 3

Paul said whatever state he was in
He had learned to be content
And he stated this very boldly,
It wasn't just a small hint.
He knew how to be abased
And he knew how to abound
And was comforted in his heart
With this new peace he'd found.
He could be both full and hungry
And he was able to suffer need,
He could do all things through Christ
Who strengthened him, indeed!
He knew God would supply his needs
According to His riches in glory,
And God will do the same for us;
That's the end of this great story.

Reference: Philippians 4:11-19

November 4

Christian, as you live your life,
As you work, and walk about,
Are you conforming to the world?
Or does your life stand out.
Are you living for Jesus?
Honoring Him and being kind;
Are you being transformed?
By the renewing of your mind;
God wants you to have courage
And strong convictions too,
To deny the world, and try to live,
Like Jesus would if He were you!

Reference: Romans 12:1-2

November 5

The Lord appeared to Solomon
In a dream one night;
He said I've heard your prayer
And chosen this as a Holy site;
If my people, called by my name,
Will be humble and pray
And each one seek my face
And turn from his wicked way,
I will hear them from Heaven
And I will forgive their sin,
I will also heal their land;
(They'd receive His grace again).
We too need to humble ourselves
And do what God told them,
We must turn from our wicked ways
And live our lives for Him.

Reference: 2 Chronicles 7:12-14

November 6

In this song David tells us
If God hadn't been on his side
When his enemies rose up against him,
It would have been like fighting a tide.
They would have swallowed him quickly
For they were filled with wrath
And they would have destroyed
All who stood in their path
But God had not given Israel
To be their enemies prey
But kept them out of their snare
And He does the same for us today.
David's help was in the Lord
Who made the heavens and earth
But ours is also in Jesus Christ
Who gave us a second birth.

Reference: Psalms 124

November 7

At the start of our new life in Christ
We're usually as "fit as a fiddle"
And at the end we're comforted
But sometimes in the middle,
We lose the joy of our Salvation
And become bored and malaise,
We lose the reality of the cross
And the joy of Jesus being raised;
Regain the joy of your Salvation
By reading God's Word each day
And be a good witness for Jesus
By living like Him along the way.

November 8

John said in the New Jerusalem,
He did not see a Temple
Because God and Jesus were there,
He explained it just that simple.
The city didn't need the sun
Or need the moon to shine.
The glory of God and Christ
Illuminated everything just fine;
The cities gates will never close
And there will be no night,
Nor will there be evil inside,
Everything will be just right.
The names of those in the city,
Written in the Lamb's Book of Life,
Shall bring God glory and honor
And cause no trouble or strife.

Reference: Revelation 21:22-27

November 9

As Christians we are sanctified;
That means we're set apart,
To live our lives like Jesus
And stay close to God's heart.
We are a peculiar people
God makes that very clear,
Different from some about us
Who have no real idea,
That unless they accept Jesus
And try to live like Him,
When that final flood* in life comes,
They'll surely sink, not swim.

Reference: Heb. 2:11
*end of ones life

November 10

John was much faster than Peter
And outran him to the tomb;
He looked inside and saw
It was just an empty room.
Peter came and went right in
But neither man realized
That Jesus Christ had risen
That's why they were surprised.
They had walked with Jesus
Yet, they did not understand
That when He was crucified
It was part of God's great plan.
There are people in our day
Scattered all across this land
Who don't believe that Christ arose
And now sits at God's right hand.

Reference: John 20:3-10

November 11

God calls us to live Godly lives
Based on what we have been taught.
Do not be conformed to the world
And the evil with which it's fraught.
The world doesn't believe in Christ
And the Scripture says they're fools.
The Bible intimidates them
For by it they are ridiculed.
Someday the world will pass away
But God's Word will always stand,
So live your life for Jesus
Who shed His blood for every man.

November 12

Paul was ignorant and unbelieving;
He blasphemed Christ and persecuted
And killed and injured Christians
For his mind had been deluded.
Yet, he thanked Christ his Lord,
Who called him to the ministry;
He who was the chief of sinners,
No one else was as vile as he.
But Paul became a role model,
Through preaching, prayers and fasting
And he won many souls to Christ,
To a life with God that's everlasting.
God gives us that same power
And bestows on us His grace,
So we can win souls to Christ
And do so in Paul's place.

Referenced: 1 Timothy 1:12-16

November 13

Christians, your testimony for Christ
Should rise up like a rocket,
Your words should flow freely
And not be kept inside your pocket.
Don't be like a firecracker
Whose fuse lights up, then fizzles,
Let your witness for Jesus
Be on fire—let it sizzle!
You'll build up treasures in Heaven
That will be put on your account
And none will be burnt in the fire.
You'll receive the full amount.

Reference: Colossians 3:23-24

November 14

More Christians should be like Zion
When the Lord's light shone on it,
They should arise and shine
Letting folks see their light is lit.
People should be drawn to us
Just like they were to Zion
And we should tell them about Jesus,
The Savior they can rely on.
The darkness that covers the earth
Will be dispelled by God's light
And then people will understand
That the Christian way is right!

Reference: Isaiah 60:1-4

November 15

In the forty fourth chapter of Psalms
It says Israel was mocked by heathens;
God seemed to have deserted them,
Yet, He did it for a good reason.
They had worshipped idols
And rejected Him and turned away
And broken His commandments
Much like we have done today.
America is now a laughing stock,
Other nations must shake their heads
For we have watered down our faith,
Our belief in God is almost dead.
No more prayer in our schools,
The Ten Commandments cast aside,
Our ways have become perverted
And we have lost our country's pride.
How long will God put up with us?
And our sinful and evil ways,
Draw us back to you, O Lord
And bless us in these days.

Reference: Psalms 44:14-26

November 16

The **last promise** in the Bible
Is when Christ said He'd surely come
And that He would come quickly,
Those were His words, the total sum.
The **last prayer** in the Bible
That brings it to an end,
Is, "The grace of our Lord Jesus Christ
Be with you all. Amen".

Reference: Revelation 22:20-21

November 17

Way back in the Garden of Eden
Adam was not deceived
But took a bite of that apple
Because of his love for Eve;
She was the transgressor
She let Satan *"do her in"*;
Adam should have protected her
But he joined her in her sin.
Wow! What a costly error
These first two humans made;
Before they committed that sin
They had it "made in the shade"!

Reference: 1 Timothy 2:13-14

November 18

Now, if you stay in God's Word
 And if everyday you pray,
Satan will surely attack you;
You will be the devil's prey.
He really hates true Christians
Who walk close to their Lord,
But you have the tool to defeat him;
It's God's Word, your two edged sword!

Reference: Luke 18:1; Hebrews 4:12

November 19

Jesus returned to Capernaum
After finishing a *"walking tour"*
And went into a local house,
He was very tired for sure.
It was then spread about the city
That Jesus had returned
And many people gathered there
To see Christ for whom they yearned.
He filled that house with glory
And for yours He'll do the same,
Just let people know He's there
And witness in His name.

Reference: Mark 2:1-2

November 20

Satan keeps going to and fro
Over this old earth, this globe,
Seeking whom he may devour,
Like he tried to do with Job
But if you do just like Job
And never once give in,
That old devil will be defeated
And every battle you will win.

Reference: 1 Peter 5:8-9

November 21

When we gather in God's name
He says that He is near,
So as we pray we know
That He will always hear,
Those prayers and petitions
We offer up for our needs
And even for a miracle,
Which God can do, indeed.
When we pray for loved ones
Who are troubled, or maybe sick,
We'd like for Him to speed it up
And answer our prayers real quick.
But God has His own time
And He does things His own way
So do not be discouraged,
Continue to trust Him and to pray.

Reference: Matthew 18:20

November 22

For the joy that was set before Him
Christ endured all that pain
And the separation from God,
Yet, He did it for our gain.
The joy set before Him
Was of sinners being saved,
Being loosed from the bonds of Satan,
Who had them all enslaved.
Yes, Jesus hung on that cross
Though He despised the shame,
To give Himself as a ransom
For those who call on His name.

Reference: Hebrews 12:2

November 23

One definition of GRACE is,
God's Riches At Christ's Expense
And when you study it closely
It really does make sense.
He gives to us abundantly
From His riches that abound,
But the best thing He has given us,
Is His Son so we're Heaven bound!

Reference: Ephesians 1:7; Philippians 4:19

November 24

Paul tells us that first of all
   We should pray prayers of intersession,
Giving thanks for those in authority
And do it with bold aggression.
Our leaders need our prayers
To rule this earth full of sin;
We must even pray for the evil ones,
That'll be for our good in the end.
This is what is acceptable
And what God says is right,
He wants all men to be saved;
We need to show them the Light.

Reference: 1 Timothy 2:1-4

November 25

To have a closer walk with God
And to be able keep in step,
You must surrender each day to Him;
The day after the night you've slept.
You must listen to Him closely
And hear what He has to say,
Then have a hunger for His Word;
He will lead you in His way.
If you'll read the Bible daily
And get on your knees and pray
You'll be able to walk with God
Each and every glorious day;
You must then deny yourself
By letting God supply your needs
And let Him live His life through you,
Being kind and doing good deeds.
Try to live your life like Jesus would,
Serving others and doing your best,
Then as you walk with God on earth,
Your life will be surely blessed.

November 26

God anointed His prophets,
In Old Testament times were told,
To talk to His children Israel
And keep them in control.
He also anointed the priests
To offer sacrifices for man's sin,
They had to be pure themselves,
Completely clean, without—within;
In these our days, however,
God speaks to us by His Word
And Christ is the sacrifice
That brings us into His herd.

Reference: Hebrews 1:1-2

November 27

When we don't pray what happens?
Our burdens don't go away,
We then become frustrated
And discouraged, day by day;
We begin to doubt the Lord
And begin to lose our joy,
We become very insecure
And subjected to Satan's ploys;
So when it comes to praying
Please don't procrastinate
But go directly to God's throne,
A later time may be too late.

November 28

There was a great gulf fixed
  Betwixt and in between,
Lazzarus and the rich man,
No one could transcend, it seems.
The rich man begged Abraham
To send someone to warn his brothers
But they wouldn't believe him;
They didn't believe Moses and the others.
Many people don't hear the truth
Even when it is expounded,
Because their hearts are hardened;
Satan's lies have them confounded.

Reference: Luke 16:25-31

November 29

Christians can do anything they want to
But their *"want to"* has been changed,
From those former sinful desires,
To which they have become estranged.
Their actions are now worthy
And no longer just worthless,
They are living for Jesus
And doing their very best;
They have a solid foundation
On which they now stand
And can do whatever they want to
But their *"want to"* is in God's plan.

Reference: Ephesians 4:17-24

November 30

Every man on earth has sinned,
Both before and after the flood,
But by God's grace we're justified
Through Christ's sinless blood;
Yes, through faith we are saved
And that faith is not our own,
Yet, that's what makes us able,
To come boldly to God's throne.
God says His grace is sufficient,
For us to overcome suffering and pain
And to get us through temptations,
When we'd much rather just complain.
Peter tells us to grow in grace
And, in faith, to remain steadfast,
Then the strength God gives us,
Will help us leave Satan in the past!

Reference: Rom. 3:24; 2 Cor. 12:9; Eph. 2:5-8
Heb. 4:16; 1 Peter 5:5; 2 Peter 3:18

December

December 1

Joshua won the battle of Jericho
 But was defeated at Ai;
This was a very small battle
And he couldn't understand why.
God gave him a great victory
But then let many of his men die;
It was because of the disobedience
Of just one very sinful guy;
This man caused others to suffer
Because of this thing he did,
Taking stuff God told him not to
And thinking it was safely hid.
When we choose to disobey God,
It will affect others within our fold
Yet He'll restore us again
If we'll do just as we're told.

Reference: Joshua 7:1-26

December 2

Elisha had a servant named Gehazi,
Who was greedy and committed a sin,
And went out and caught Naaman
Who then reeled his chariot in.
Gehazi told him that his master,
Wanted both silver and clothes
But this was a very big lie,
Elisha wanted none of those.
Naaman gave him what he asked for
And his men helped take them home,
Then Gehazi lied to his master,
Who knew what was going on;
Elisha's spirit was with Gehazi
When Naaman stopped his chariot
And gave him what he asked for
And now this will be Gehazi's lot;
Naaman's leprosy will cling to him
All his life wherever he goes,
So when he went out from Elisha
He was a leper as white as snow.
This servant couldn't fool Elisha
About the silver or the clothes
And we can never fool God
Because He knows all—He knows!

Reference: 2 Kings 5:20-27

December 3

God gives each man a free will
But only to a certain degree,
For if he had full control
He would live mostly in misery;
He would chase after his wants
Instead of seeking basic needs
And he wouldn't learn to trust God,
His heart would be filled with greed.
But man does have a free will
And can do most anything he wants
But things he does not pleasing to God
Will always come back to haunt.

Reference: 1 Peter 2:15-16

December 4

Elisha's miracles stayed around
After he was dead and gone,
For a dead man's life was restored,
When he touched Elisha's bones;
That man stood on his feet
When he came to life again
And we may have that same effect
When our lives come to an end;
If other people see Christ in us
As we live our lives each day,
They may become alive in Christ
Even after we've passed away!

Reference: 2 Kings 13:20-21

December 5

When we do good works on earth
　　　Let them be for God's sake
And then we'll be rewarded
With crowns which we will take,
And do with them as the elders did
In Revelations where we're shown,
They cast the ones they earned,
At the feet of Jesus at His throne;
The elders said, you are worthy Lord
To receive honor, glory and power,
For you have created all things,
(That includes time, every hour).
We know you made us O Lord,
To give you joy and pleasure,
So may the works we do for you
Be so great they're hard to measure.

Reference: Revelations 4:10-11

December 6

Those who say God dislikes money,
　　Are making a really bad call
For He is the true source of it
And is the owner of it all.
Money is one of God's blessings
That should be put to good use
By being generous to others,
Avoiding greed and abuse;
Let it not make one conceited
Or be the object of their hope
For it can cause many snares
And temptations with which to cope;
If one uses money wisely,
By seeing it from God's aspect,
They'll be concerned for eternal things
And therefore have the Lord's respect.

Reference: 1 Timothy 6:17-18

December 7

In the third chapter of Psalms,
Those that troubled David increased
And many rose up against him
And his soul was ill at ease.
Some say there was no help from God
But Lord you were his shield,
And the lifter of his head;
How good that must have made him feel.
When we have those that trouble us
And can find no peace within,
We too must cry out to God
And He will also lift our chins.
Our eyes will not be downcast
In those days of our despair,
We can hold our heads up high
For we know that God is there.
He's the one who gives us strength
In our times of pain and trouble
And as we learn to rely on Him
Our blessings He will double.

Reference: Psalms 3

December 8

One day Elisha journeyed
Through a city named Shunem
Where a good woman lived
Who offered bread to him
And each time thereafter
As he traveled through
He went into her house
Like she wanted him to do;
Her husband built him a room
Then put in a bed and stool
And a candle to give light,
Also warmth when it was cool.
She took real good care of him,
So he would give her a reward;
"All I want now is a son",
Is what she told this man—her lord.
Elisha then did a miracle,
For her husband was very old,
He gave her the son she wanted,
This to her was better than gold.
This woman took care of Elisha
Who was God's man of the hour
And if we'll do that for His man today
Many blessings on us He'll shower.

Reference: 2 Kings 4:8-17

December 9

God told Obadiah in a vision
The city of Edom was despised,
For they thought they were great;
This is what they surmised.
They were prideful and deceived
For since their city was up high
They thought no one could conquer them
But God proved this was a lie.
They exalted themselves as eagles
And set their "nest" among the stars
But God brought them down to earth,
Away from their "Jupiter and Mars";
We must not have an attitude
Of superiority and pride,
Like those people in Edom had
And expect God to be on our side.

Reference: Obadiah 1:1-4

December 10

A master gathered his servants
And said to these three men,
I am going on a long journey
Take care of this till I come again.
To the first he gave five talents;
Today that would be five "grand".
To the second he gave two talents
To keep safely in his hand;
He gave one talent to the third man
And hoped when he returned,
That each of these three men,
Would have more money, earned.
The man with five had five more
And the man with two had double
But the third man hid his talent
And was now in lots of trouble;
The master praised the first two men
But was angry at number three
For if he had put it in a bank
It would have earned him usury.
Are you a good steward of the money
God has entrusted to your care?
If you are God will bless you
And give you more than your share.

Reference: Matthew 25:14-27

December 11

One day a great woman's son
Went to his father in the field;
This boy had a terrible headache
And the pain was just unreal.
He was taken to his mother
And sat on her knee and died,
Then she went out to find Elisha
And it doesn't say she ever cried.
Elisha then went to her house
And prayed, and laid on this lad,
Then put his mouth, to his mouth
Breathing into him the breath he had.
Was this mouth to mouth resuscitation?
No, it was a healing very Devine
And the boy opened up his eyes
After sneezing seven times;
This lad's mother loved Elisha
And had cared for him many days,
She knew he could heal her son
So she really was not even fazed.
If we could love God like that
And really be convinced,
That He can still do miracles,
It would sure help our confidence.

Reference: 2 Kings 4:18-37

December 12

If we break one Commandment
We are guilty of breaking them all
And we cannot justify ourselves
By saying the one we broke was small.
We must know that telling a lie,
Is to God, the same as stealing
And even loose, idle gossip
Someone's character may be killing.
Yet, God forgives each of those sins
And tells us they're forgotten,
It doesn't matter if they're small,
Or really big and rotten!
God wants *us* to forgive those
Who sin against us one and all
And remember their sins no more
But it's up to us to make that call.

Reference: James 2:10-11

December 13

As Paul preached a long sermon
A young man up in the loft,
Went to sleep and fell out a window
And his landing was not so soft.
Paul hurried down to this man
And saw that he was dead,
Then fell down and embraced him
And to those around him said,
Do not trouble yourselves
This man's life is still in him,
So they broke bread and ate
And Paul talked till dawn with them.
Paul said goodbye and departed
And the people were very sad,
Until the young man woke up
And they were comforted and glad.
This tells us that sleeping in church
Is more dangerous than one expects,
So it behooves us all to stay awake
And give the preacher his due respect.

Reference: Acts 20:7-12

December 14

Elisha now had a sickness
That would soon cause him to die,
So King Joash went to see him
And this king began to cry.
Elisha said go get a bow and arrows
And he put a hand on top of his,
Then said open the window and shoot
And Joash made the arrows whiz.
Elisha was testing this king's faith
To see if it was great or small
The arrows would be God's deliverance
From Syria once and for all;
He told Joash to go get the arrows
And beat them against the ground;
Which Joash did three times
And this made Elisha frown;
He should have struck them six times
To prove his faith was strong;
He now must fight Syria three times,
For what he did was wrong.
He would have fought them only once,
Had his faith been strong, not weak
And our own battles will be easier
When our faith is at its peak!

Reference: 2 Kings 13:14-19

December 15

God told His children, Israel
He'd be there and give them rest;
He said if they would yield to Him,
He'd see that they were blessed.
When we, too, have a yielded heart,
We'll be convicted when we sin;
Our conscience will be clearer
And our hearts made pure again.
Our faith will be much stronger
When we are in God's will
And our lives will bear more fruit
As we are Spirit filled.

Reference: Exodus 33:14

December 16

This is about those two thieves,
Who beside Christ, were crucified;
Each went to a different place
The moment that he died;
One thief ridiculed Christ,
Acting just like the crowd,
That scorned and mocked Him
And His deity disavowed.
That thief would go to Hades
Where he'd spend eternity
In Satan's lake of fire
And never would get free.
The other thief believed in Christ
And knew He was God's Son,
He would be with Him in Heaven
Once his suffering was done.
Now no one gets to Heaven
By any good works they do
But only by what Jesus did,
When He died for me and you.

Reference: Luke 23:32-43

December 17

When the Virgin Mary greeted her
Elizabeth's unborn baby boy,
Who would be John the Baptist,
Leaped in her womb for *joy;*
Christ brought *joy* to Simeon
Who did not want to die,
Until he saw the Son of God
With his very own two eyes.
Christ brought *joy* to the disciples
When He calmed the angry sea
And *joy* to blind Bartimaeus
When He caused this man to see;
The sick, the lame and the weary
Were filled with *joy* and very glad
As was His friend Lazzarus,
Raised from the dead, not smelling bad.
Jesus brought *joy* to many others
Yet those *joys* seem diminished
By His ***ultimate joy*** on the cross,
When He said... ***"It is finished"!***

Reference: verses from Mark, Luke, John & Hebrews

December 18

God tells us in the Scripture
He loves a cheerful giver
And that He will send His blessings
Like a mighty flowing river.
When you give willingly
It's for your sake alone
And He'll reward you greatly
For your obedience has been shown.
Yes, when you give freely
God will let His blessings flow
And He'll give back to you
More than you'll ever know.

Reference: 2 Corinthians 9:6-8

December 19

If a woman lost just one,
Of her ten silver coins,
She would seek it diligently
Because she would be forlorn;
Yes, she would be so miserable
That a candle she would light
And she'd sweep her whole house
To find that coin ere comes the night.
She'd call her friends together
Once that lost coin was found,
Then they'd rejoice together
And happiness would abound.
This parable about the lost coin
Is about what it represents
And that is great joy in Heaven
For one lost sinner who repents.

Reference: Luke 15:8-10

December 20

Are you heavy laden
And somewhat down trodden?
Do you feel all alone
Like you have been forgotten?
Then God has news for you
He says come, I'll give you rest;
If you'll cast your cares on Him
He'll give you His very best.

Reference: Matthew 11:28

December 21

All Christians should be grateful
They don't have to suffer like Paul,
For the persecutions they endure
Do not compare to his at all.
Five times he received lashes
Of thirty nine strokes, it's known;
He was beaten with rods three times
And one time he was stoned.
Three times he was shipwrecked
And was day and night in the deep,
He was in dangerous waters often
And you know he lost much sleep.
Paul faced the perils of robbers
And of his own people, no less;
He faced dangers in the cities
And out in the wilderness.
He was often cold and hungry
And naked and in great pain,
But everything he endured
Was strictly for God's gain!
To keep from getting captured
He was lowered down by a wall,
So when we compare our trials to his,
They suddenly seem very *small!*

Reference: *2 Corinthians 11:23-33*

December 22

Listed here below
Are some *"I AM's"* of Christ:
I *am* the Messiah,
I *am* the Bread of Life,
I *am* the light of the world,
And I *am* the door,
I *am* also the way,
And there's even more;
I *am* the truth and life,
Christ also says that *I'm*,
The Alpha and the Omega,
And *I am* the true vine,
I *am* the Son of God,
I *am* the Good Shepherd too;
I know my sheep by name,
(He sure hopes that includes *you*)!

Reference: various verses in John; Rev. 1:8

December 23

Josiah became a king
  When he was eight years old;
He walked in God's ways
And did great things we're told.
Years later the king of Egypt,
Necho was his name,
Was called to fight a battle for God,
But Josiah also came.
God told Josiah through Necho
This was not his fight, don't meddle,
But Josiah didn't listen
So things became unsettled.
Josiah even disguised himself
In order to fight this king
And he got wounded and died,
(He was caught up in death's sting).
Josiah obeyed God most of his life
But this time he said, I won't;
If you ever decide to disobey God,
Think about Josiah—and **don't!**

Reference: 2 Chronicles 35:20-27

December 24

Before the birth of Jesus
Zacharias and his wife
Would have a child of their own
That would really change their life.
Elizabeth and her husband
Were righteous, without blame;
They kept God's Commandments
And they glorified His name.
Gabriel appeared to Zacharias
And said to him fear not,
Your wife will bear a son,
You'll call him John—that's what!
Zacharias was old, so he doubted
And was instantly struck dumb,
Not able to speak at all,
As if his mind was numb.
When Elizabeth had her baby boy,
She said John would be his name,
The people couldn't believe it
Till Zacharias wrote down the same;
Since he no longer doubted God
The very moment that he wrote,
His mouth opened and he praised God
And the people all took note.
This shows God could do anything
He wanted to way back then;
To not believe He can do it today
Would be an awful sin!

Reference: Luke 1:5-80

December 25

It came to pass in those days,
Caesar Augustus sent out a decree
That everyone would be taxed
And no one dared to disagree.
Joseph went to his hometown,
The city called Bethlehem,
And his wife Mary, great with child,
Made that long trip with him;
Jesus was born in that city
Wrapped in swaddling clothes,
Long and narrow bands of cloth,
For Mary had plenty of those;
She laid Christ in a manger
Since there was no room in the inn,
This precious baby lay there,
Who would take away man's sin.
A host of angels appeared
To shepherds in the field,
Saying glory to God in the highest
And on earth peace and good will.
The shepherds hurried to Bethlehem
To see that which had come to pass
Then made known what was seen
And they spread the word so fast.
Those who heard their story
Were amazed and filled with wonder,
Yet, when Mary heard their sayings,
She kept them in her heart to ponder.
Yes, over two thousand years ago
Christ our Savior was born;
It was such an awesome birthday,
We celebrate it every Christmas morn.

Reference: Luke 2:1-21

December 26

Jesus was a man of prayer,
   For many times He went out
To be alone, all by Himself,
With no one else about;
He said we should also pray,
Desperately and fervently,
Much like the way He prayed
In the Garden of Gethsemane;
Much like He prayed on the cross
While hanging there in shame,
Asking God to forgive us,
As He shouldered all our blame;
Our prayers should be persistent,
We must keep asking, seeking, knocking,
And God will answer those prayers,
Sometimes in ways so shocking;
Our prayers must show reverence
Toward God the Holy One
And must recognize God's purpose,
That is, His Will be done.
We should pray for our needs
Asking Him for our daily bread,
Then rest in the expectation
He will hear the words we've said.
Put your faith to work by praying,
Don't keep it on a shelf
And don't always just pray for "stuff";
Ask God to fill you with Himself.

Reference: Luke 1:1-4; 22:11-42; 23:34

December 27

Christians are stronger and taller
When on their knees in prayer,
Where they have access to God
And can all their burdens share.
We don't go through anyone
Other than Jesus Christ, God's own,
In order to talk to God freely
And meet Him at His throne.
Isn't it an awesome thing
We can talk to Him one on one?
And know if we trust Him fully
He'll say, my child well done.

December 28

To reject the virgin birth of Christ
Is like calling God a liar,
For when He sent Christ to earth
Salvation of man was His desire.
You can't believe His Word fully
If you disbelieve the whole idea,
That Jesus was born of a virgin;
Scripture makes that very clear.
God put Christ in Mary's womb
To bypass the sinful blood of man;
This was prophesied by Isaiah,
Yet, some still don't understand.
Christ's blood had to be perfect,
Not from Adam, that man of sin,
This is so very important
It must now be said again.
Joseph was of Adam's blood
That was handed down to man,
So the virgin birth is no myth,
It's the very core of God's plan.

Reference: Isaiah 7:14; Matthew 1:18-25

December 29

The empty grave is the guarantee
That when Christ died for you and me,
He did not stay in that tomb
But was later seen in the upper room;
Many saw Him on that cross
Where He died to save the lost;
His disciples thought this was the end,
They didn't know He'd rise again.
Once they realized this truth,
The empty tomb became their proof,
That Jesus was alive once more
And that opened up a door,
For them to preach the Gospel now
And joy returned to them somehow.
They now knew that Christ arose
And would tell this fact to all those,
Who would listen to their story,
They praised God and gave Him glory.
Today the Gospel message thrives
Because Jesus lives—He is alive!

Reference: the four Gospels

December 30

God made it clear to Jonah
That He wanted Nineveh saved
But Jonah didn't agree with Him
And he deliberately disobeyed.
He was told where he should go
And exactly what he must do
But since he hated the Ninevites
He did not follow through.
Jonah found out very soon
That you cannot run away;
God knows where you are,
Every minute of the day;
Now getting away from God
Was really Jonah's wish
But all he did was to end up
In the belly of a fish!
We cannot run away either
For God is everywhere
And when He gives us an order,
We'd better do it then and there.

Reference: Jonah 1:1-17

December 31

When we're chastised by God
It really is not a fluke,
For He tells us in His Word,
Those He loves He will rebuke.
When we chastise *our* children,
We say something that's so true,
And God must say the same thing;
"This hurts me more than it does you"!
Yes, our God is a loving God
Who is always good and kind,
When He put Christ on that cross,
He had *us* on His mind.
Let us live our lives for Jesus
And if in sin, let us repent
And God will be proud of us,
As will Jesus, whom He sent.
God loves us so very much
It's really hard to comprehend
That His love is unconditional
And eternal—without end!

Reference: Revelation 3:19

Other books by the Author:

A Little Boy and His Trains

Published by Xlibris
48 pages of pictures and true stories about a little boy and his love of trains, and some of the adventures he and his grandfather shared together.
www.xlibris.com
www.amazon.com

Bible Stories in Rhyme and other poems

Published by Victory Graphics and Media, Tulsa, OK
180 pages of famous, and not so famous, Bible stories put to rhyme, and other poems.
www.biblestoriesinrhyme.com
www.amazon.com

To contact the Author
E-mail: geecrum@bellsouth.net
Phone: 770-957-3286

LaVergne, TN USA
17 November 2009
164330LV00003B/1/P